The Danish Smorrebrod
The Ultimate Dinner Party!

Complete Instructions on the Rules, Order and Recipes

By
Kim Sorensen

Table of Contents

Table of Contents

Dedication

In Canada, we have a melting pot of cultures. I'm 100% Danish, although born in Canada to Danish parents, my kids are 1/2 Danish, their kids are 1/4 Danish and their kids will be an 1/8 Danish. This book was written to preserve one of the most loved of all Danish Traditions... THE DANISH SMORREBROD. You will also find an amazing collection of some of our best Family Danish Recipes. Of all the Danish traditions, I believe the Danish Smorrebrod tradition is one of those traditions that should be preserved for future generations. You don't need to be young or old or Danish to put on a Danish Smorrebrod. Anyone can put on a Danish Smorrebrod. I don't ever remember a guest who wasn't throughly impressed with the drinking, eating, fellowship and fun time and at the end, was so thankful to be a part of such an event. The idea to write this book came to me after one of my very successful (7 hour) Smorgs. My nephew Jeff came up to me afterwards in the kitchen and told me I needed to write everything down in a cookbook so that his generation would know how to put on a Smorg. So this cookbook is written for those future generations, who want to host a proper Danish Smorrebrod (Smorg), but weren't sure how to put one on and to everyone else, I promise you... if you buy this book and follow its rules and content, you will experience the best dinner party ever!! This book was a long time coming... but here it is!

Dedication

Some of the people that have inspired this book are my Grandma (Mormor), Sigurd Stoyberg, my Grandfather (Farfar), Alfred Sorensen, my mom (Mor), Doris Sorensen and I have to include Peter Christiansen from Calgary's Danish Canadian Club. So I dedicate this cookbook to all of them as well, for it is they, who have taught me the rules and most of the recipes in this cookbook.

My mom's favourite grace when she was growing up was...
"Dear God... Thank you for the food before us... the family and friends beside us... and the love between us... Amen!"

Introduction to The Author

I was born in Calgary, Alberta on October 18, 1952, the eldest of 5 siblings. I think I always loved food, beginning when I was a kid, staying with my grandma on the farm in Raven, Alberta. We ate the freshest vegetables and many hand picked berries from her garden and surrounding countryside. My memories are the pancakes with the very heavy cream and sugared berries... or the best potato soup ever! There was also the cinnamon buns, the white dinner buns, her sand cake and banana cake and her legendary brown bread. I remember whenever it would hail in the summer, grandma would run out and get pailfuls of hail to make ice cream. Home made ice cream... oh boy, it was good! But my love of Danish food started at home in Acme with my mom and Farfar working together in the kitchen. Farfar was a great cook, who would do most of the planning and cooking as mom was working outside the home. Every Christmas was very much Danish too with the celebration starting on Christmas Eve... Roast Duck, Goose or Pork Roast with the crackling! Dessert was always the Risalamande and the appropriate number of almonds nuts hidden in the pudding for us kids to find.

Living in Denmark, after high school, brought more experiences and love for the Danish food and culture. Then it was back to living with my grandma in Calgary while going to University. At grandma's, her cooking was simple but oh so good. I considered it very healthy eating, at least before she started bringing out her baking.

It was during my time in Calgary, that I started going to the Danish Canadian Club and met Peter Christiansen. I also joined the Danish Businessmen's Association in the 1980's and once a month, I enjoyed many spectacular Danish meals and Smorrebrod's. Today I get such a thrill cooking great food and pairing it with the right wines and beer. I love going the extra mile, because of the thrill it gives my guests. The totally satisfied smiles on their faces tells the whole story and that is the only reward I need for my efforts. My favourite Danish Tradition is the Smorrebrod or Smorg as we call it in my family. I love to see my guests enjoying the fellowship of the other guests and enjoying multiple courses of tasty Danish delights. I've had a couple of very special moments that will stay with me forever. The first one, is when a young danish friend of my son (Axel) by the name of Kasper, came to our house for Christmas Eve. He was visiting from Denmark and was very home sick, but when he walked into our house, I had just put on the red cabbage... he took about 2 steps inside the house, stopped and breathed in deep, then in a loud voice, full of emotion and with a giant smile, said "now that's the smell of Christmas"! That really made my day! The second one, was when I had a full on Danish Smorrebrod, Den Yule Stort Bord (The Christmas Big Table). This was a 7 hour (5 to midnight) very successful Smorg that had great food, many akvavit and beer and many great laughs. It was so much fun, that at the end of the evening, my nephew, Jeff came up to me, got my attention by grabbing my shoulders and looked me straight in the eye and said "now that's a f*#king Smorg"!! You don't know how good that made me feel.

Story Page

It's the perfect response that rewards me for all my efforts! So, I hope this book will inspire people to preserve and carry on this wonderful Danish Smorrebrod Tradition. Start planning soon and enjoy this cookbook called "The DANISH SM0RREBR0D... Vrersgo"!

....

Below find a picture of myself, Danish Canadian Club General Manager Peter Christiansen and the Danish Baker George Nielsen in the Mermaid Inn at the Danish Canadian Club.

Akvavit

It would be a mistake not to say a bit about how important Akvavit is to the Danish Smorrebrod. Akvavit is produced from grains and potatoes and flavoured with a variety of herbs but mostly caraway. The first known reference to Akvavit came from a Danish Lord who wrote a letter and sent a sample of first known Akvavit to the last Roman Catholic Archbishop of Norway, dated April 13, 1531. The sample was described as "some water which is called Aqua Vite" which is very helpful for all sorts of illness which a man can have both internally and externally. A common asked question is, "is it spelled Akvavit or Aquavit?" Well it's Akvavit! This is the Danish way to spell it. The Germans, French, Dutch and English spell it Aquavit. There are also other spellings, all similar but different. Regardless of how you spell it, it's pronounced the same... "Akvavit"! Generally, Akvavit is poured in one ounce shots and drank all in one gulp and always with friends or family, never alone. It's almost always drank with beer and with food. It would seem strange to see someone in a bar just drinking Akvavit alone. It is a very special social drink, that is shared at celebrations such as Smorg's, Christmas, Easter, Summer Holiday and special meals., but truth be told, the Danes like to drink it anytime, but always together with family or friends! One of my early Akvavit memories was when my Farfar and I were visiting family in Copenhagen. Farfar and his brother in law, Inar, would start first thing, every morning before breakfast, with an Akvavit snaps with a couple of drops of bitters! So there's proof that you can enjoy it anytime!

Introduction to the Smorrebrod

For the Danes, there is nothing more special like attending a Smorrebrod. It is a popular event that was originally put on during Christmas day or Boxing Day, but today it has expanded to include birthdays, anniversaries or just about any special occasion. You almost always receive your Smorrebrod invitation well in advance and when you walk into the host's home, you are immediately visually reminded about how special the rest of the day is going to be. The guests are all smartly dressed, the house is ready and the table is set beautifully... and yes, you should now be bursting with excitement and so ready for the evening! The term Smorgasbord is actually a Swedish term with the Danish term being Smorrebrod (buttered bread) or Kolt Bord (cold table) or Den Stort Bord (The Big Table).

Today, here in Canada, our family simply use the term "Smorg" but with a difference. Instead of the food being put on the table all at once, buffet style, the Danes will bring out the food, course after course of food in strict order for an extended period of time (2 to 7 hours). No matter what you call this event, the Danes have their rules and a specific order for the food to be brought out. The essence of a real Smorg is all about taking your time to eat and talking to your guests as you share food, conversation and time. Granted, there is a lot of food, but we spend many hours eating it. No Smorg ever took an hour... and there is no time limit on how long we might sit there. A Danish Christmas Smorg can easily take an entire afternoon and continue right into the evening with some experiencing quite a hangover the next day. This is why the bigger Smorgs are usually done during the holidays, such as Christmas, Easter or Summer holidays. This is when people have more time to relax and enjoy food, snaps and company to the max... and appreciate the following extra day to recuperate. Although all Smorg's start with the pickled herring, the host determines the length of time and the number of courses served. A short Smorg could be 2-3 hours and full on long Smorg could be 6-7 hours. Your choice and yours to organize as the host.

All Smorg's are special and have their roll out order, but, as a rookie, it's tricky to know how much to dish up during a smorg, especially when they haven't told you that there are 7 more courses to follow the one you're eating... and what foods go together. Can you put remoulade on liver pate? (answer: no) and do you ever put herring with prawns? (answer: NEVER). How much Akvavit are you allowed to drink? Answer: As much as you can, but not so much that you appear drunk. Rookies will fill their plate like they are at a Swedish "all you can eat" buffet. They will also hit the akvavit hard not realizing there are many more shots to come. Despite the advice, you just know that some won't last till the end. Many a rookies have left the table after round 2 and never to be seen again. The biggest and best Smorg of the year is at Christmas. This is called the "Den Stort Julbord" (The Big Christmas Table) and is also the one that takes the longest to complete. There are many dishes and rounds and there will absolutely be lots of beer and akvavit... and not to forget the many toasts and singing too! What ever Smorg you organize, big or small, it is always a very special dinner party! Skal!!

The Rules, Order And "How To" Of A True Danish Smorrebrod!

Rule #1 - To the host the Seating Order is always important. You can use name cards and strategically place each of your guests in the place you want. So if you already have your own seating arrangements thought out, then disregard the following method of seating I use. I never sit husband and wife together and I never sit the same gender together. I find couples will have way more fun and join in on the conversation if they are separated. When I call out "vrersgo" for everyone to take a seat, I always do so with the instructions, "boy girl boy girl, and don't sit beside your spouse". Plain and simple, it has worked brilliantly!

Rule #2 - It is customary for the host to do the first toast at the very beginning just after everyone has been seated. This should include a welcoming to your home, thanking everyone for coming, a reminder to put your cell phones on silent and put away, acknowledging the first time Smorgers (rookies), the number and order of courses (a reminder about how to pace yourself), announce to everyone, that if they wants to honour you, the host, to please stand and give at least one toast during the evening... and lastly but most important, to have fun!

Rule #3 - Always use your best table manors and always eat with knife and fork... NEVER touch the food with your hands. (See the Table Manors section)

Rule #4 - Always start with herring and remember it needs its own plate as it is a strong pickled tasting fish and you don't want to taste those flavours while eating all the other foods. .... so make sure to remove the herring plate with a clean one and replace if necessary.

Rule #5 - Although Akvavit goes great with all the Smorg courses, it goes particularly well with herring. ....so make sure to have plenty of shots with this first course   and yes you're suppose to drink the whole shot.

Rule #6 - "EVERYONE" should give at least one proper toast during the evening. It can be a thank you or a joke or any witty statement. A proper toast starts by clinking your glass before standing up. Once you have stood up, you should hold your glass chest high and close to your chest and then say your toast. Once you have completed your toast, hold your glass away from your chest but still no higher and it is important to look everyone in the eye, before saying "skal"!! Never raise your glass above your face!

Rule #7 - At your Smorg it is traditional and best to serve Beer and Akvavit, but you can serve wine instead for those that can't tolerate beer or prefer wine. It is a known fact that Akvavit pairs amazingly well with all the different Smorg foods and Danish beer (Tuborg, Faxx and Carlsberg). ....but not all Smorg foods goes well with wine or anything else. If possible, stick with Danish beers or any lighter tasting beers... they're the best for smorgs..........definitely not strong alcoholic beers or strong tasting Pale or IPA beers.

Rule #8 - The order of the food always stays the same   but the number and selection of courses can vary depending on how big or small you want your Smorg to be. It is always herring first, followed by other cold fish dishes such as egg and anchovies, shrimp, caviar, lox, smoked salmon... followed by warm fish, soup and warm meats... followed by cold sandwich meat and cheeses, fruit and finally by dessert. Salad is the wild card and can be placed anywhere among the warm dishes. For the benefit of all, but particularly the rookies, the host should announce what each course is as it is placed on the table. I will give you an example of a few suggested Smorg menu plans on the next page.

Rule #9 - Generally, the Danes do not make up Danish Open Face Sandwiches in advance and served. Why, because Danes know how to make up there own sandwiches and just the way they like it. Plus you do not know what type or how many sandwiches your guests will want. Sandwiches are very personal and VERY filling... so it is best to put each of the sandwich type and all the associated condiments on their own platter and let the guests make their own up. The rookies can always ask for help from the veterans. Now with that said and considering a future full of rookies at your table, you could make up a selection of beautifully garnished open face Danish sandwiches and place them on the table. Some of these sandwiches are very easy to make, while others can actually be layered with so much amazing foods and garnishes. There's literally nothing more beautiful than an Open Face Danish Sandwiches... and simply put... it makes for amazing eye candy on your table. Just saying and your choice.

Rule #10 - In our family and generally speaking, the beer should be served ice cold and the Akvavit should come right out of the freezer before pouring.

Rule #11 - Every guest should always thank and compliment their gracious hosts and not just once. Remember, the hosts have probably put their heart and soul into planning and making the food, decorating the house and the table and maintaining a steady flow of food, beer and akvavit through out the day. This is not a backyard burger event, but the ultimate invitation to a very special event. It is customary to bring flowers, akvavit and/or a gift for the hosts, but just not food. When you look back at how much fun you had that day, and you will, remember, it was the hosts that made that day happen... so thank them many times!!

Rule #12 - This last rule is about honouring the Danes! If you're going to call it Danish "Smorg" or "Smorrebrod", make sure you honour your ancestors and strictly follow the smorg rules. Danish Smorgs are fun and special because of the rules. So if you're not going to follow the rules, then call it a Swedish dinner party or anything else, but not a Danish Smorrebrod (Smorg)!

Suggested Smorg Menu Plan

A good Smorg should be well planned, days ahead of time and then executed as planned on the Smorg day. Smorgs are all about great food, not fast food or homemade vs store bought. The following is a basic menu plan I have used many times and that I base most of my Smorgs on, today. If you follow this The Big Smorg (Stort Bord), it will take you about 7 hours to complete. You can shorten the smorg time by eliminating courses from this full on smorg plan. So ask yourself, how long do I want my Smorg to last? Most of the food can be prepared ahead of time, especially the condiments like pickled beets and cucumber (Asier and Agurksalat) and side dishes like red cabbage. Remember, homemade is always better than store bought, so make your condiments and side dishes well in advance (check out the condiment recipes inside).

Here's the order of food to be strictly observed at the Smorg.

1 - pickled herring

2 - cold seafood and egg

3 - warm seafood, warm meat dishes and salads

4 - cold sandwich meats, cheeses and fruit

5 - dessert

Akvavit and beer is served through out the Smorg with all of the courses, with the exception of the dessert... where an aperitif such as Danish Cherry Liqueur, Sherry or Port should be offered.

THE BIG SMORG (STORT BORD) 7 hrs

First Course - 5 PM Rye Bread

Regular, Spiced and Curried pickled herring 5:25 PM

Remove and replace (if necessary) all pickled herring plates White and Rye Bread

Eggs, mayonnaise, parsley, snap herring or anchovies, caviar 5:40

Baby shrimp, mayonnaise, dill sprigs, caviar, and lemon wedges 6:00

Lox salmon, sweet spicy dill mustard or scrambled egg, red onion, radish wedges, capers, dill sprigs and lemon wedges.

Second Course - 7:15

Plated fried filet of sole on shredded lettuce with remoulade, parsley sprigs, lemon wedges (I like to add on top a couple shrimp and caviar as garnish) Third Course - 8:00

Plated Clear Soup with parsnips, carrots, leaks, meat balls, dumplings and garnish with a sprig of fresh Parsley

Fourth course - 8:45

Plated Tarteletter with chicken, asparagus, peas and carrots.

Fifth Course - 9:25

Plated Frikadeller (2), boiled potatoes and white stewed cabbage Sixth Course - 10:00

Plated Medister Sausage (3 inches), candied potatoes, dark gravy and red cabbage

Seventh Course - 10:45 Sandwich meats and cheeses...

Tray #1- LEVERPOSTEJ (Danish liver pate), pickled beets, red cabbage, pan fried sliced mushrooms, bacon pieces,

Tray #2- TILSET and HAVARTI cheese, thin sliced green peppers, red onions and grapes.

Here you can add more types of sandwiches to this seventh course if you want such as:

1- HAM with ITALIAN SALAD,

2- ROAST PORK with the crackling and red cabbage.

3- ROAST BEEF slices with remoulade, grated horseradish and agurksalat.

Be aware of how much your guests are going to be able to eat. Sandwiches are very filling.

FYI... just know there are so many combinations and types of danish sandwiches for your choosing... it's endless!

Eighth Course - 11:30

Danish Apple Cake or Risalamande or Kransekake

For shorter Smorg's, you can simply serve fewer courses. Our family seems to be into the "big" special occasion Smorgs, but Smorgs do not have to be a big event with lots of people. You'll do more smorgs in a year if you include small group ones. For example, all Smorg's must have and start with herring (even if you have just one kind)... but then after that you add what you want as long as the order is honoured. I had a great mini Smorg with my 90 year old mom. We had the following 1 hour lunch smorg:

1 - Curried herring on rye.

2 - Levepostej (Liver Pate) and pickled beets on rye

3 - Citron Fromage (Lemon Pudding) for dessert

The following 3 hour lunch Smorg was with 2 other couples...

1 - regular, spiced and curried pickled herring on rye

2 - egg, snap herring and caviar on rye

3 - shrimp, mayo, caviar, dill sprig, lemon wedge on white bread

3 - Emma's honey curried spinach salad

4 - Chicken and Asparagus Tarteletter

5 - leverpostej, tilsit cheese, fruit and nut bread and grapes

This was a perfect smorg for a Saturday or Sunday lunch. The courses are endless, you decide how much you want to serve and that determines how long the smorg will last. Just remember all smorg's must have and start with herring. After that, add some beer and Akvavit and the courses you want, while maintaining the order... and just like that, you have a Danish Smorg!

Family Style or Plated?

I need to take a moment to discuss whether to serve your courses family style or plated. As the host, it's your choice and should be part of your grand plan. At the Danish Canadian Club in Calgary and in Denmark where everybody is Smorg experienced, the food is mostly served family style. This is because after the host has explained in his welcome speech, how many courses are planned, experienced smorgers know how to pace themselves. However, I have seen even experienced Danes so uncomfortable and full after 3 courses, they had to go home. They simply were too excited and dished up way to much food early on. Unfortunately, they went home, skipping the last 4 courses and the rest of the evening as well.

This is embarrassing to both the guest and the host. You can't serve everything plated, but you may want to help your guests control their urges and plate some of your courses for 2 reasons. ONE, you can show off your plating talents by placing beautifully plated courses in front of your guests and TWO, you can help your guests control the amount of food they consume with an appropriate portion. While, most will thank you, the rest can ask for seconds! Just don't fret about the garnishing and plating... yes it is an art... but it's easy and fun to do.

Just remember to follow the order and decide what you want to serve... family style or plated or a combination... and then just do it... that's it!

Table Manners

Let's just talk about eating etiquette for a moment and why it's important to be displaying your best manners at a Danish Smorrebrod. The simple answer is to make the practise of eating with others, a pleasant, respectful and in a sociably acceptable manner. What maybe pleasant and comfortable to you at home, can be distracting to others. No one is offended by good table manners, so why not use good table manners at a special Danish Smorg event? It's why parents are encouraged to eat at home with their children everyday, using and practising these sociably acceptable manners and etiquettes. Once started and practised, it will soon becomes a habit. SO NOW, you're invited by invitation to a very special dinner event. So the least you can do is display and show off your best manners so as not to be a distraction. Here's my take on what to remember when you're invited to a Danish Smorg.

1-	The first thing is to turn off your cell phones and do not lie them on the table but put them away completely out of sight. If you must check your cell for calls and texts wait until you are finished a course and have moved far away from the table. People's obsession for their cell phones today is becoming an epidemic and sends a message to your host and guests that your cell phone is more important than the conversation and food at your table. It's just rude! Surely, we can do without the cell phone for one evening.

2-	Never sit down at the table until your host has asked and explained how to do so. Then take your designated seat and sit straight up in the chair, pull it comfortably towards the table, so your hands and wrist can lay comfortably on the table... never place your elbows on the table.

3-   Here is the simple silverware and dinnerware rules. Bread plate to your left, drink glasses to the right. Any food dish to the left is yours, and any glass to the right is yours. Start eating with the knife, fork, or spoon that is farthest from your plate, work your way in, using one utensil for each course. Your host has it all planned and will most likely explain this as the evening progresses.

4-   Table manners have evolved over centuries to make the practice of eating with others pleasant and sociable. Keep these basic, but oh-so-important table manners in mind as you eat.

-Chew with your mouth closed.

-Hold utensils correctly (opposite if left handed). Fork in the left hand, knife or soup spoon in the right hand. Never put your utensils back on the table once you have used it. Always rest your utensils on the plate. If your utensils are resting at 4 and 8 o'clock, it means do not take your plate away as you are not finished... if your utensils are both resting at the 4 to 5 o'clock positions, it means you are finished and your plate can be taken away. See pictures.

-To use your napkin start by placing it on your lap. Then when you need to use your napkin, take your napkin and use one finger to dab at your lips. Never use a closed hand on your napkin and wipe your mouth like you would wipe a table. If you have to temporarily leave the table, never place your napkin on the table or your plate, place your napkin on your chair and push your chair back to the table. If the host announces the meal is finished, place your napkin folded neatly beside your plate. Never place your napkin on your plate.

-Wait until you're done chewing to take a drink or speak. Never speak with food in your mouth.

-Pace yourself with fellow diners. Cut only one small piece of food at a time.

-Avoid slouching and don't place your elbows on the table while eating.

-Instead of reaching across the table for something, ask for it to be passed to you. If someone asks for the salt, always pass both the salt and pepper together. They should never be parted.

-Leave your plate where it is when you are finished with your meal-don't push it away from you.

-You may leave the table, only after the host has signalled the meal is over.

Utensils at 4 and 8 o'clock means you're not done eating.

Both utensils at 4 o'clock means you're done eating.

How to Set a Table for a Danish Smorrebrod

Table Setting is a very important part of the Danish Smorrebrod. It sends the "special" message to your guests and sets the tone for the event. No Danish Smorrebrod was ever served on paper plates! At a Danish Smorrebrod, your table is as important as the food. With that said, from a small to large Smorg or a two hour to a six hour Smorg... the rules for table setting are the same. Table setting can be simple or complex, but there should be always a nice table set ahead of time for when your guests arrive. The art of table setting is actually simple once you understand a few basics. So put the effort in and set a beautiful table and treat your guests to the full experience.

First we need to make some decisions on what plates and utensils we want to use for each course, as this will determine how we will set the table. We also have to keep in mind how many plates we have at our disposal and how much washing plates and utensils we want to be doing in between courses while the Smorg is on. So let's get started... first question is are we using charger plates to put our other plates on? We could use a regular dinner plate instead of a charger plate that we could actually use for one of our course(s) like the second course after the herring plate is removed. We know we must use a separate herring plate for the pickled herring and replace it with a clean plate as soon as that course is done but that clean plate could be the regular dinner plate that the herring plate was on. Then are we using one regular dinner plate for the rest of the first course and/or as a charger plate for other plated courses we'll be serving? If we're using a plate as a possible charger plate at least at the beginning, the other plates we place on top, could be for the soup, tarteletter, fish fillet, frikadeller and medisterpolse courses and so on. So those plates we could bring to the table with each of the above courses. Also, how many sets of spoons, knives and forks are we using for the evening, including the herring dishes, soup, warm, cold dishes and dessert? We'll need a soup spoon and other knives and forks for the rest of the courses including the cold meats and cheeses. We'll also need a dessert spoon or fork and a coffee spoon. It is important to plan this a head of time, while keeping in mind how many and what type of plates and utensils you have at your disposal, so simply, take the time to plan out the plates and utensils and be organized before your smorg. Ok we're ready to begin setting the table.

First, we begin by laying out a crisp tablecloth. Then we could place a regular dinner plate with a herring plate on top to start. We can place on the right side of the plates, a soup spoon, knife and knife. On the left side of the plates we can place two forks. On top of the plate we will place the fork or spoon for the dessert and the spoon for the coffee. This set up could be what the host had planned if you were supposed to use one knife and fork for the herring. The host would clear the herring plate off with the knife and fork. Then you would use the last knife and fork for the rest of the evening. However, you can plan to use a fresh knife and fork for every course.

There's no rules for how many knives and forks you place on the table. However, it would look silly to have 7 forks and 7 knives along each plate. So use some common sense and decide accordingly.

On the top right corner of the plate, you can place a beer glass, a schnapps glass and water glass. The coffee cup and saucer is generally offered at the end of the courses and brought out at that time.

Never have unused plate settings or extra chairs around a table.

I'm not going to tell you not to use "actual" Charger plates but generally they are not used at a Danish Smorrebrod. Also, the bread plate at the top left corner is nice to have if there is room, especially for the herring and cold fish courses... but the bread plate can be optional.

Fold the napkin (or use a chic napkin ring) and place it on top of the herring plate. If using name cards, place a name card above the place setting with the appropriate guest's name on both sides so they can find their seat and the guests on the other side of the table will know who they are talking to.

Place your centre pieces on the table. Make sure it is not too high (8"-10" max) or it will interfere with your guests seeing who's across from them. Multiple salt and pepper, butter and condiments can be placed on the table too.

Marnie and Kim Sorensen October 2020.

Note

Cook's notes

We need to have a conversation about salt. I come from a family that is not afraid to use salt. In some of the recipes, I have indicated the amount of salt to add, so that you don't have to guess and continue adding and tasting for the right seasoning. Okay, I recognize that some people might not like as much salt as I do... so if you prefer, you can take a bit off the measurement in the recipe... but I recommend trying the recipe first as instructed. Just saying...

...

Below was a small birthday smorg with some friends and family at the Danish Canadian Club October 2021.

Main Course

Crispy Pork Belly with parsley sauce - Stegt flresk med persillesovs

,Stegt flcesk med persillesovs, Crispy Pork Belly with parsley sauce is Denmark's National Dish. This dish is served with or without the rind. If you want the rind still attached to the pork belly, you will probably have to order it, otherwise, you can find pork belly without the rind in grocery stores.

Pork Belly

700g (1 1/2 lbs) pork belly

salt and pepper generously

Parsley sauce

25 g (2 tbsp) butter

3 tbsp all purpose

flour 1 cup milk

1/4 cup cream

2 cup (25 g) diced parsley

pinch freshly grated or

ground nutmeg

1/2 tsp salt

1/2 tsp white pepper

Pork Belly... Preheat oven to 450°C. Cut the pork belly lengthwise into 1/2 inch widths. Heavily salt and pepper both sides and place on a baking tray lined with aluminum foil in the middle of the oven. After about 20 minutes turn the pork belly over and salt and pepper again. Place back in the oven for about 15 min more before removing from the oven onto a plate and paper towel, before serving. The pork belly should be slightly crispy and dark golden brown on both sides.

Yield: serves 4 I Recipe by Kim Sorensen

Crispy Pork Belly with parsley sauce - Stegt flresk med persillesovs

Parsley Sauce... Melt the butter in a pot, then add the flour and mix. Slowly add the milk and cream, until the sauce has a nice creamy texture. Add the parsley, salt, pepper and nutmeg and simmer for 3 minutes and serve. Serve the pork belly and parsley sauce with boiled potatoes and the vegetable of your choice.

Danish Apple Pork - !Ebleflresk

This is a very traditional Danish Dish and is very simple to make. You can also use thick sliced bacon instead of pork belly... just don't add salt to the bacon.

**4 tart apples cored
and sliced lengthwise
2 medium onions
sliced lengthwise
6 slices meaty 1/4 to
1/2" thick pork belly**

**1 tbsp sugar
1 tbsp fresh
thyme leaves salt
1 tbsp fresh thin sliced
green onions**

Using a frying pan, fry the pork belly until the fat is rendered, it has turned to a nice brown colour and slightly crisp. Sprinkle liberal amounts of salt on both sides while frying. Don't over cook the pork belly or it'll be too hard. Place the pork belly on a plate with some paper towel. Leave the grease in the pan and fry the onions and thyme with some salt till golden brown. Place the onions on another plate with some paper towel. In the same fry pan now put the apples, sugar and some salt and fry til they are golden brown. Place lots of apples and onions on a slice of rye bread before placing 2 slices of pork belly on top garnished with some green onions slices.

Yield: makes 6 sandwiches or serves 6 I Recipe by Kim Sorensen

Danish Apple Pork - Æbleflæsk

Danish Meat Cakes - Frikadeller

Frikadeller is one of the most recognizable foods in Denmark and there are many slight variations to this recipe and that's why it's very common to hear a Dane say ,my mother makes the best Frikadellers,.

Old Farfar (Alfred) liked the texture of his pork meat ground fine, so he would send it through the meat grinder 3 times. If you don't have a meat grinder, you can ask your butcher to grind some pork meat up through his meat grinder three times. I ask for pork shoulder with enough pork fat to make up a regular grind blend. I also like the original Danish recipe of all pork frikadeller, but it's common today to use a combination of pork and beef, even all beef. Alfred would also sometimes use either chicken or beef broth instead of all milk. This recipe is a close reflection of my Farfar's Frikadeller recipe, although he never used a recipe. He ground most of his pork at home himself with the onions... then Farfar would quarter the meat and onions in a bowl, so he would have 314 meat1onion mixture and 114 empty space . He would then fill the empty 114 space with flour and from there he would add milk, eggs, salt and pepper until he had the right texture. He often would make the mixture up in the morning and leave it sit in the fridge till he was ready to fry just before supper. It wasn't until recently I learned how important it is to let this mixture sit for at least an hour before frying. Today, you simply have to buy a pound of ground pork from the grocery store and use the blender to prepare this meal, thus making this recipe so very easy to make.

1 kg (2.2 lb) Ground Pork

240 g (1 large Onion) Onion 60 g (1/2 cup) Flour

122 g (1/2 cup) Milk

100g (2 large) eggs

2 tsp Salt

2 tsp Pepper Butter for frying

Yield: 38 - 40 Frikadeller I Recipe by Kim Sorensen

Danish Meat Cakes - Frikadeller

Place the ground pork in a large mixing bowl. Then in a blender set at the lowest speed, add the milk, egg, flour, salt and pepper. Lastly add the onions and stop mixing once the onions have been mixed. You want it mixed coarse but not pureed. Pour the mixture into the mixing bowl with the ground pork. Mix well until there is no clumps of ground pork. Your mixture should be a very soft. Let this mixture sit in the refrigerator for at least an hour (preferably 2 to 3 hours) before frying. Using the palm of your hand and a large spoon (dipped in cold water) make a small egg shaped frikadeller. The cold water will keep the pork from sticking on the spoon and your hand. Fill the fry pan quickly and fry slow on medium heat before flipping each of them over. Alfred used a fork to flip the frikadeller in the frying pan, You need to have lots of butter or oil in your pan and have the right amount of heat so your frikadeller don't burn.

Your frikadeller should ideally be flipped only once, fried golden brown on both sides and just cooked in the middle. Serve immediately with boiled potatoes, stewed white cabbage and the vegetable of your choice.

Danish Meat Cakes - Frikadeller

Danish Fish Cakes - Fiskefrikadeller

You can use any fish for this recipe plus you don't have to add the salmon, but the salmon makes for a beautiful rich looking fiskefrikadeller. The dill and capers makes this danish otherwise you could call this a fish cake.

454 g (1 lb) cod fish
60 g (2 1/2 oz) salmon
diced (1/2 cm sq.)
1 egg
180 g (3/4 cup) heavy
cream 42 g (5 tbl) flour

zest from 1 of lemon 70
g (1/2 cup) shallots
a good handful of
chopped dill 10 g (1
tbl) of chopped capers
3/4 tsp salt
3/4 tsp pepper

Using a food processor or blender pulse coarsely the cod, cream, flour, egg, shallots, zest, salt and pepper. Pour the mixture in a large bowl and mix in the salmon, capers and dill and let the mixture stand for an hour before frying. Using your hand and a spoon, make Frikadeller size portions and fry in butter on medium heat. To prevent burning, make sure you have enough butter in the pan. Serve fishcakes with Remoulade, buttered potatoes and a cucumber salad!

Yield: Serves 4... makes 16 fiskefrikadeller I Recipe by Kim Sorensen

Fish Frikadeller

Chicken and Asparagus Tarteletter - Tarteletter med kylling og asparges

These are delicious puff pastry shells that are filled with a creamy combination of chicken and asparagus. Dating back to the beginning of the 20th century, this Danish classic can be enjoyed as an appetizer, a light main course, or part of a Danish Smorg table. The puff pastry shells can be bought from most grocery stores in the freezer section. We use Tenderflake puff pastry shells with lids - 6 to a box. The traditional recipe calls for white asparagus, but since it is not readily available, you can use green asparagus instead... and although you can use fresh white or green asparagus, many Danes will use the white asparagus from the jar that can be bought in most European deli stores... plus you can use the juice from the jar to make your roux. This gives the Tarteletter an enhanced asparagus flavour. There is approximately 314 cup of liquid in the 530 g jar of white asparagus, so I use 1 114 cup of chicken broth to make up my 2 cups of liquid needed for the roux. If you are using fresh asparagus, then boil the asparagus in a little water until the asparagus is soft. Use the water and broth to make up the 2 cups of liquid.

1 cup (150 g) chopped
cooked Chicken
1/4 cup (4 tbl) Butter
1/4 cup (4 tbl) Flour
2 cups (480 g) of Chicken
broth and asparagus juice

1 cup (300 g) of 2 cm
chopped well cooked
Asparagus
1/2 cup (85 g) frozen Peas
and Carrots
1 small handful of Parsley
1/2 tsp of Pepper
1/2 tsp of Salt

Yield: 20 Tarteletter I Recipe by Kim Sorensen

Chicken and Asparagus Tarteletter - Tarteletter med kylling og asparges

In a pot, make a roux by melting the butter and then add the flour. Slowly add the asparagus and broth liquid and continuously whisk until the roux is a thick consistency. Add the chicken, asparagus, peas, carrots, salt and pepper and mix well. Put an appropriate amount into each of the tarts. Garnish with a parsley sprig and serve.

Danish Meat Balls in Curry Sauce - Boller i Karry

This is a dish that Farfar served us when we were growing up in Acme. Farfar used to place a small dish of curry and water concentrate on the table if anyone wanted to add more heat and spice. Also, I love the curry sauce with the chunks of apples, however, you can also blend the sauce using a hand blender if you prefer a smooth consistency.

The Meatballs:

500 g (1.1 lb) Lean Ground Pork 200 g (7 oz) 1 Onions quartered

130 g (250 ml) Flour

145 g (150 ml) Milk

1 (60 g) large eggs

1 3/4 tsp Salt

2 tsp Pepper

The Curry Sauce

200 g (7 oz) onion, diced 150 g (5 1/4 oz) apple diced 2 1/2 tbsp curry

4 tbsp all-purpose flour

2 1/2 cup chicken or beef broth

3/4 tsp salt

2 tbsp (28 g) butter

fresh parsley sprigs for garnish

The Meatballs: Place the ground pork meat in a large bowl and set aside. In a blender, mix the onions, milk, egg, salt and pepper at the lowest setting . As soon as it starts blending, take the cap off and add the flour into the blender and continue mixing at the lowest setting just untill the flour has completely mixed in. Pour the mixture into the bowl of ground pork and mix together well. Set aside in the fridge for 1 - 2 hours.

Yield: 6 persons I Recipe by Farfar and Kim Sorensen

Danish Meat Balls in Curry Sauce - Boller i Karry

Fill a large sauce pan with water (3/4 full) and bring to a medium boil. Place a small spoonful of the pork mixture onto your wet hand and then using your other hand, roll the mixture between them into a small one inch round meatball and place into the boiling water. When the meatballs float to the top, remove them to a bowl. The meatballs can be made a day ahead of time.

....

The Curry Sauce:. Fry the diced onions and butter in a large sauce pan for about one minute. Add the curry and fry for another minute. Add the diced apples and fry again for another minute. Add the flour and mix everything together until the flour is completely soaked by the moisture from the apples and onions. Add the broth and salt. Let it simmer uncovered on low heat for 15 minutes until you have a nice thick sauce. Finally, add the meatballs to the sauce and let them heat up for about 5 minutes. Serve the curried meatball mixture hot with some rice and a sprig of parsley for garnish. You can serve this meal with a veggie and/or side salad.

Danish Meatballs in Curry - Boller i Karry

Fried Fillet of Sole - Filet af Sål

Filet of Sole - Filet af Sal

This is the recipe I use for the Danish Smorg fish course. The most important tip I can give you is to use medium heat and lots of butter so you don't burn the fillets. Flip them only once and they should be golden brown on both sides.

6 filet of sole

All purpose Flour egg

fine bread crumbs

butter and

vegetable oil salt

and pepper

Organize your three containers... a shallow bowl for the egg(s) and two shallow plates one for the flour and one for the bread crumbs. Now pat dry each filet and lightly flour both side of the fillet (make sure to shake excess flour off) before submerging them in the egg and then finally coat both sides with the bread crumbs. The order is always flour, eggs and bread crumbs. Fry the coated filets in a fry pan with LOTS of butter and vegetable oil, set at medium/high heat. Salt and pepper both side to taste. The heat should be set so that the filets quickly so that they are golden brown on the outside and just cooked on the inside.

For your smorrebrod, place the fillet on top of shredded iceberg lettuce and garnished with a dollop of remoulade, lemon wedges and dill sprigs. This fillet can be served with boiled potatoes and parsley sauce. This is also the fillet used in making the special Danish sandwich "Shooting Star".

Yield: Yields 6 portions I Recipe by Kim Sorensen

DANISH ROAST PORK WITH CRACKLING - DANSK STEGSVIND MED KRAKKELING (FL!ESKESTEG)

Danish roast pork with crackling is one of the most traditional Danish dishes that you can make. It's also very popular and traditional at Christmas time. Tip: Since you are working with an open roasting pan, make sure your broth doesn't evaporate and dry out... so continue to add water. This will ensure the best gravy!

2 kg Boneless Pork Loin pork roast with rind on

coarse salt

1 litre broth (pork, chicken or beef)

1 carrot sliced

1 onion sliced

1 small bundle of thyme Salt for the rind

Use a sharp knife to cut long deep grooves in the rind of the pork roast. The grooves should be about 5 mm (1/4 inch) apart. Make sure to make deep grooves in the rind but do not cut into the meat. Rub the entire roast thoroughly with coarse salt making sure to get some salt in the grooves. Place the roast on a rack with a roasting pan underneath. In the roasting pan; add 1 liter (4 cups) of water or preferably broth (pork, chicken or beef) and some sliced carrots, onions and a small bundle of thyme. This water with the vegetables can later be used to make a nice gravy. Make sure that the roast is lying in a horizontal position. You can use.

DANISH ROAST PORK WITH CRACKLING - DANSK STEGSVIND MED KRAKKELING (FL!ESKESTEG)

a ball of aluminium foil under the roast to level it. If you do not do this you risk getting the rind an uneven color or even burnt. Preheat the oven to 440 F and cook the roast for 20 minutes. Turn down the heat to 400 F and continue cooking for about 1 1/2 hours depending on the roast size or until the core temperature is 135 F. Make sure to add more water as there will be a lot of evaporation during the roasting. This will ensure a great gravy. If you need to crisp the kraken a little more, you can turn on the broiler. But if you use the broiler, make sure the roast is level and keep a close eye on it and don't burn it. When the roast is done, take it out of the oven and rest for about 10 minutes, then slice the roast at each groove. If you want to make a nice gravy; strain the vegetables from the roasting pan water and then separate the fat from the broth and pour the remaining broth in a sauce pan. Add some broth and heavy cream and some brown gravy coloring. Add salt to taste and thicken if desired.

Yield: 8 -10 persons I Recipe by Kim Sorensen

DANISH ROAST PORK WITH CRACKLING - DANSK STEGSVIND MED
 KRAKKELING (FLÆSKESTEG)

Danish Meatloaf (Mock Hare) - Forloren Hare

This is a traditional Danish recipe. What sets this recipe apart from the others is that it is made with bacon and a very unique tasty gravy that goes with it.
My grandma Stoyberg made a meatloaf similar to this, but instead of putting bacon on top, she tops it with tomato soup instead.

454 g (1 lb) Ground Pork

454 g (1 lb) Ground Beef

230 g (1/2 lb) finely diced onion 1 egg

3 tbsp (18 g) bread crumbs

1 tsp mustard

1 tsp ground ginger 1 1/2 tsp salt

1 1/2 tsp pepper

8 slices of thin bacon 1/2 cup of heavy cream 2 tbsp all-purpose flour 2 tbsp butter

1 cup of beef broth

1/4 cup of red currant jelly

1/2 tsp gravy browning

In a large bowl mix the ground pork and beef together well with the onion, egg, bread crumbs, mustard, ginger, salt and pepper. When well mixed, place in an 8" x 4 1/2" x 2 1/2" greased baking pan. Pat the sides down and round up the top. Now place the bacon strips on top of the meatloaf. Here's where you interlock the bacon (4 strips - 4" and 4 strips - 8") for the weave design. Pour the heavy cream around the edges and place into a 350 degree convection oven for at least 1 hour. Take out of the oven and carefully lift.

Yield: Yield 6 Portions I Recipe by Kim Sorensen

Danish Meatloaf (Mock Hare) - Forloren Hare

the meatloaf up and onto your serving board and set aside to rest while you make the gravy. Melt the butter in a fry pan, then whisk in the flour. Pour the liquid from the meat loaf pan into your fry pan roux and continue to whisk. Add the red currant jelly and then the beef broth until the roux is the desired gravy texture. Add the gravy browning for the desired deep brown gravy look. Serve with Hasselback potatoes and the vegetable of your choice. Make sure to save a slice or two of meatloaf for your sandwiches the next day, if there's any left over!

Danish Pork Meat Patty - Karbonader

This is a very traditional danish meal. Some use a little veal in the meat mixture, but my family like it with just ground pork. This is traditionally served with creamy white sauce with peas and carrots and potatoes. The pan drippings left can be used as a sauce for the Karbonader. This meal is a favourite family meal for many Danes.

450g (1.0 lb) ground pork

1 egg

1 cup bread crumbs

salt and pepper to taste 1/2 cup of butter

Make 4 tall oval meat patties - 4 oz each. Set up 2 small bowls... one with a well whisked egg and into the other bowl put the bread crumbs. Season the outside of each patty with salt and pepper, then dip into the egg bowl and then into the bread crumbs. Make sure the patties are breaded on all sides. Fry the Karbonader in medium heat until dark golden brown and just cooked in the middle. Use a meat thermometer (150 F) if you can. If it is a little pink in the middle it is perfect. Season to taste while it is frying. Serve with White Sauce with peas and carrots, boiled potatoes and the vegetable of choice.

Yield: Yields 4 Karbonader I Recipe by Kim Sorensen

Danish Pork Meat Patty - Karbonader

Pork Tenderloin in cream sauce with onion & Mushrooms with Baked Potato Chips - Morbradboffer i flodesauce

This is an old Danish dish that is deliciously easy to make. You can also use any jelly if you don't have cranberry jelly.

450 g (1 lb) pork tenderloin 1/2" steaks

3 tbsp all purpose flour

Salt/Pepper for seasoning

225 g (1/2 lb) butter for frying 250 ml (1 cup) boiling water 11 g bouillon cube

600 g (1.3 lbs) 1/4" onion rings 450 g (1 lb) mushrooms sliced thick

250 ml (1 cup) heavy cream

900 g (2 lbs) 5 mm sliced potatoes

oil for brushing

50 ml (1/5 cup) cranberry jelly

BAKED POTATO CHIPS. Brush the potato chip slices on both sides with lots of oil and place the potato slices on a baking sheet lined with parchment paper. The potato slices should not be layered.

Sprinkle with salt then bake in oven for 25 min at 400 F degrees. Turn them over once they start to brown or after 15 min, but don't let them burn! You'll know they are finished when they are crispy and golden on the outside and still slightly soft on the inside.

Sprinkle with a bit more salt and serve them hot.

Yield: serves 6 - 8 I Recipe by Kim Sorensen

Pork Tenderloin in cream sauce with onion & Mushrooms With Baked Potato Chips - Morbradboffer i flodesauce

PORK TENDERLOIN. Mix well, the 1/2 " Pork Tenderloin slices with the flour in a bowl or plastic bag until the steaks are well coated with flour. Fry the steaks in plenty of butter and season well with salt and pepper on both sides. When golden brown remove the tenderloin steaks from the fry pan and store on a plate. Then in the same pan, fry and season the onions, with more butter, salt and pepper. Once caramelized and golden brown, remove and store on the plate with the steaks. Again in the same fry pan, add the mushrooms with more butter, salt and pepper. You want the mushrooms to be barely cooked (2 min) before adding the onions back into the fry pan. You should have used all the butter by now.

Mash the bouillon cube into the boiling water before adding the water to the pan. Remember to scrape the bottom of the pan. Add the tenderloin steaks back in the fry pan and simmer for 5 minutes. Pour in all the cream and let the sauce thicken. Season with salt and pepper.

Pork Tenderloin in cream sauce with onion & Mushrooms With Baked Potato Chips - Morbradboffer i flodesauce

if needed. Lastly add the cranberry jelly and mix well. Serve the tenderloin steaks with the potato chips and a green salad.

DANISH PORK STEW - (M0RBRADGRYDE)

This is an old traditional Danish stew. It's very tasty! Tip: Use any small tasty cocktail wieners or cut up larger wieners... but make sure they are tasty!

1 (450 g or 1 lb) pork tenderloin cut in bite size pieces

150 g (5 oz) bacon chopped

150 g (5 oz) mushrooms thick sliced

150 g (5 oz) cocktail wieners whole

540 ml (2.3 cups) chopped tomatoes and juice

300 g (11 oz) onions chopped

150 g (5 oz) carrots chopped

150 g (5 oz) celery chopped

2.5 dl (1.06 cups) heavy cream 1

1/2 tsp paprika

1 1/2 tsp salt 1 tsp thyme

1 tsp ground black pepper

In a large saucepan, fry the bacon and onions till cartelized, then add the carrots, celery and mushrooms and continue to fry for a couple of more minutes. Add the tomatoes, cocktail wieners, heavy cream, paprika, thyme and salt and pepper. Let the stew simmer for 30 minutes then add the pork tenderloin and simmer for 10 minutes more.. Serve hot with rice or mashed potatoes..

Yield: serves 8 I Recipe by Kim Sorensen

DANISH PORK STEW - (MØRBRADGRYDE)

Danish Sausage - Dansk Medisterpolse

If you're talking about Danish Sausage, then you're talking about Medisterpulse. It's simple to make, but oh so delicious. You can grind your own or just buy regular grind pork hamburger from your local store. The more fatty the grind the better and less dry the sausage. Don't use lean pork! Tip: Two ways to cook Medisterpolse... 1- Boil the sausage till its just cooked, then fast fry in butter till just browned on both sides... 2- Don't boil the sausage, just use lots of butter and oil and slow fry the sausage til they are completely cooked through and golden brown. Your choice. Either way, don't overcook the sausage!

1.5 Kg (3 1/3 lbs) regular pork hamburger

150 g (1/3 lb) lard (broken into cubes)

500 g (1.1 lb) onions (halved and quartered)

50 g (1/4 cup) potato flour (or all purpose)

3 egg whites

3/4 tsp ground nutmeg

1 1/2 tsp allspice

1/2 tsp ground cloves 2 1/2 tsp salt

2 1/2 tsp pepper

600 g (2 1/2 cups) pork broth (beef or chicken)

2 meters (approx.) pork casing

First soak your casings in water. Then place the broth, lard, onions, cloves, nutmeg, allspice, egg whites, salt and pepper into your blender. Blend at the lowest setting till the mixture has just blended. Then, while still blending, lift the lid off and add the flour and continue to blend just till the flour has blended through. A coarse blend is what you're looking for.

Yield: 8 - 10 servings I Recipe by Kim Sorensen

Danish Sausage - Dansk Medisterpolse

In a large bowl, vigorously mix together the pork hamburger and your mixture. Rest in the fridge for an hour while you get your sausage stuffer casings organized. Using your sausage stuffer, stuff the pork mixture into the into the casings firmly without air bubbles. Cut into long sections (1 1/2 to 2 ft) and place into freezer bags for freezing. When ready, cook the sausage, using either tip method, till golden brown.

Serve with mustard (Sennep) and Danish red cabbage and boiled potatoes.

Liver, Onions, bacon and mushrooms in rich gravy - Lever, log, bacon og svampe i rig sons

This is one of those comfort foods you grow up loving and wish you could eat everyday! This is one of my favourite recipes! Tip# 1 cut or buy your liver thick sliced. Tip# 2 cooking the onions, mushrooms and bacon slowly to prevent burning, will ensure a better gravy.

600 g thick sliced liver
400 g thick sweet onion
rings 1/2 cup of butter
Flour for the liver and
gravy Beef Broth

Beef bullion cube Thyme, sage
for gravy (optional)
25 g thick sliced mushrooms 120 g
thick bacon
Salt and Pepper to taste

Place your thick sliced liver in a bowl. Add milk, enough to cover the liver and place bowl in the fridge for an hour. In a large fry pan with medium heat, melt 1/4 cup of butter. Add sliced onions, lightly season and fry until golden brown. Then remove to a covered warming plate to be placed in the oven 160 C.
In the same pan, fry the mushrooms until just soft and lightly season. You may have to add more butter. Remove to the warming plate with the onions. Again in the same pan fry the bacon not too crisp. Place the not too crisp bacon on to the warming plate with the onions and mushrooms. Cover the warming plate and put in the oven to keep warm. Remove the liver from.

Liver, Onions, bacon and mushrooms in rich gravy - Lever, log, bacon og svampe i rig sons

the milk wash bowl and pat dry then lightly flour each side. Place the liver in the same fry pan used above.

Lightly season with salt and pepper. Don't pour any of the liquid out and add more butter if needed. Fry the liver at medium heat until golden brown but don't overcook. I like to fry till the internal temperature is 160 F. If some of the liver is still slightly pink, you've fried your liver perfectly. Remove liver and place in the warming oven on a separate plate covered. Once you remove all the liver pieces use the pan and all the juices to make the gravy. Add more butter if needed to make a good roux. Using a whisk, add 2 tbsp of flour to the pan juices, then add beef broth till the gravy is to the desired thickness. Add thyme, a bit of the bullion cube and salt and pepper to taste. Place one or two pieces of liver on a warm plate, top with the warm onions, mushrooms and bacon. Serve with a green vegetable and mashed parsley potatoes with a large pool of gravy. Make sure you have extra gravy on the table for those that will want more.

Yield: Yields 2 - 4 portions I Recipe by Kim Sorensen

Yes the thick sliced liver is under the toppings!

Roast Duck with apples and prunes stuffing - Duck med rebler og beskrerfyldning

Roast Duck is very popular and traditional at Christmas time. This recipe will produce a tender well done duck with tasty crisp skin.

DUCK
1 - 6-7 lbs (3 kg) whole duck 3 cups of chicken broth
1 small bunch of fresh thyme
salt and pepper
STUFFING

3 - (500 g) apples, skin on quartered
40 - (250 g) prunes cut in half
1 - (300 g) large onion chopped
1 tbsp butter
2 tbsp fresh thyme leaves Salt and pepper to tasted

Remove the giblets, neck and wing tips from the duck. Clean and rinse the duck. Cut off some of the excess neck skin and fat leaving enough skin to close cavity and place these skin pieces and excess fat in a large fry pan. Set the duck aside while you work on the stuffing. Heat the fat and skin for a couple of minutes to melt the fat before discarding. Then add the butter, apples, prunes, onions, thyme and season with salt and pepper. Stir and cook with medium heat for just a few minutes. Rub the outside of the duck liberally with salt. The salt will help crisp up the skin. Now stuff the duck cavity with the apple prune stuffing using a spoon. Close up both ends of the duck with.

Roast Duck with apples and prunes stuffing - Duck med rebler og beskrerfyldning

toothpicks, metal needles or thread to hold the stuffing inside the duck. Cut off the wing tips and place the wing tips, giblets, neck and a small bunch of thyme underneath the grill in your roasting pan. Add the broth before placing the duck in your roasting pan with breast side down. Sprinkle a little more salt on the back of the duck before putting it into the middle rack of the oven at 300 F for 2 hours. Then turn the duck breast side up and sprinkle more salt on the breast and roast for 2 hours more. It's the salt that will crisp up the skin. After at total of 4 hours, remove duck and let sit for 10 minutes, while you make the gravy. Remove and strain the broth into a pan. Using a turkey baster and tipping the pan, remove as much of the clear duck fat as you can... or a much simpler way is to use a fat/broth separator. Bring the broth to a boil and thicken to your liking with flour and hot water shaken well in a container. Season to taste, but taste it first as depending on how much salt you used on the duck, it may not need any more salt, maybe just some pepper. Now remove the stuffing from.

Yield: Yields 4 - 6 I Recipe by Kim Sorensen

Roast Duck with apples and prunes stuffing - Duck med rebler og beskrerfyldning

duck to a serving bowl and cut off both leg and thigh and both breasts leaving the crispy skin on.

Depending on the portion sizes wanted, the breasts can be cut in half, thus producing the 6 portions. Best served with candied potatoes and red cabbage and your vegetable of choice like brussel sprouts.

Danish Cabbage Rolls -Fyldt Hvidkalshoved eller Rouletter

This is an old danish style cabbage roll recipe that Farfar loved. It's made with the white sauce instead of the rice and tomatoes. The juices from the cabbage and meat mixture blend so well with the sauce, it makes a very tasty meal emphasizing the cabbage and meat.

1 small head of cabbage MEAT MIXTURE

454 g (1 lb) ground lean pork

454 g (1 lb) ground lean beef 250 g (1 cup) milk

150 g (1-2) carrot shredded

270 g (1 medium) onion diced 1 cup chopped fresh parsley 1/4 cup chopped fresh dill

150 g - 3 - 4 eggs

1/2 cup bread crumbs

1 tbsp salt

2 tbsp pepper SAUCE

3 tbsp of butter

4 tbsp of flour

reserved cabbage water 50/50 milk, heavy cream salt to taste

Remove the cabbage outer wilted leafs and remove the stem. In a large covered pot, place the cabbage, stem side down in 2 inches of boiling water (4 cups of water) for 2 minutes. Gently remove only the loose outer leafs that you can before placing the cabbage back into the pot for another 2 minutes. Try not to rip the leafs when removing. Repeat this process until all the large useable leafs are removed.

Yield: Makes 26 cabbage rolls or fills 2 - 8" x 8" baking dishes I Recipe by Kim Sorensen

Danish Cabbage Rolls -Fyldt Hvidkalshoved eller Rouletter

Cut out the stem from each leaf by making a V cut and then place all the separated leafs and the remaining head that is left back into the covered pot to cook for 5 minutes. The leafs should be flexible enough to wrap around the meat. Reserve the remaining cabbage pot water (1 - 2 cups) in another container along with the remaining small cabbage head for the sauce. In a large bowl, mix the ground meat, milk, shredded carrot, diced onion, parsley, dill, eggs, bread crumbs, salt and pepper. Put a large spoonful of meat mixture in each lettuce leaf and roll it up and stuff both ends with the excess lettuce ends. Wrap to make a nice size cabbage roll and cut off any excess leafs. Place each roll fold size down, side by side and fill your oven proof baking dish. In the large pot, make a roux using the butter and flour. Roughly blend the reserved water and remaining cabbage and then add the mixture (approximately 1-2 cup) to the roux. Continue by adding some milk and heavy cream to end with a very thick white cream sauce.

Season with a little salt and pepper and pour the sauce over the cabbage rolls. Place the baking dish in the 350 F oven for one hour and serve.

Danish Cabbage Rolls -Fyldt Hvidkålshoved eller Rouletter

English Steak - Engelsk Bof

This is Farfar's recipe. Farfar also used on many occasions, horse tenderloin cut 314, thick. Horse meat is common in Europe, but not in Canada. So today, you would do the same recipe using beef tenderloin cut 1 - 314, thick (6 0z) for each piece and no pounding. Pounding meat is necessary for cheaper cuts of tough meat like Round Steak. To add a little exotic flavour to your gravy, you can add some fresh thyme and rosemary sprigs... then remove the sprigs when ready to serve.

1 1/2 lbs round steak (4 - 6 oz pieces 1/2 in thick)

1 large Onion sliced

2 tbsp of Vegetable Oil

1/2 cup butter

1 tbsp corn starch or flour

Pound each piece of steak thin and season with salt and pepper. Then place in a hot fry pan with the oil. Sear both sides, then reduce the heat and add the butter. Once the steak pieces are cooked to your liking, let the steak sit for 5 minutes while you fry the sliced onions golden brown. Remove the onions and make the gravy by thickening all the juices in the same fry pan, with the flour. Serve steak, onions and gravy immediately with boiled potatoes and the vegetable of your choice.

Yield: 4 servings I Recipe by Farfar

Pickles

Pickled Beets - Syltede Rodbeder

Others may like a different mixture, but our family likes the 50150 sugar vinegar mixture. Make sure your lids are new or in good shape, otherwise your beets can spoil. To lessen the chance of spoilage, only make as much pickled beets as you can use in a year. Instead of slicing the beets you can also quarter them or the real small beets from your garden can be pickled whole.

3 Kg raw beets (with a bit of stem and root left on)

3 cups white sugar

3 cups white vinegar

3 - 1 litre sterilized pickling jars

Put all the beets in a large pot and fill with water covering the beets. Slow boil till the beets are just cooked. Don't overcook the beets otherwise the texture will be too soft. Drain the water and set aside to cool with lid off so it doesn't continue to cook in the steam. When cool enough to handle, using your hands, peel off the beet's outer skin under the cool running water from your kitchen tap. When all the skin is removed, use a large knife to cut off the root, the top of the beet and any visible bruises on the beet. Now slice the beets in 1 - 2 cm slices or the size of your choice. Leave the very small ones whole. Cut any of the slices in half that are too large for the mouth of the jars.

Yield: 3 - 1 litre jars of finished pickled beets I Recipe by Kim Sorensen

Pickled Beets - Syltede Rodbeder

In a large pot, add the sugar and vinegar and bring to a low boil. Fill the jars with beets and then fill each jar right to the top with the sugar vinegar mixture. Screw the lid on and shake until all the air has risen to the top. Then remove the lid and fill the jar to the top again. Put the lid on and tighten with your hands only. Rinse the jars under the tap to clean the outside and mark the month and year on the jar. Store in a cool dark cupboard until you're ready to use. Can be ready to use in only a week.

Pickled Cucumber - Asier

If you sterilize both the jars and good lids well, you should be able to store these for months in a cool dark cupboard.

2 large cucumbers (2 lbs) 1 1/2 cups of sugar

1 1/2 cups of regular vinegar

1/2 teaspoon mustard seeds 1/2 teaspoon dill seeds

1/2 teaspoon black pepper corns

Sterilize jars and lids in boiling water. Peel cucumbers. Cut in half and scoop the seeds out. Cut the cucumbers lengthwise slightly shorter (1") than the height of the jars and in 3/4" strips. Lay the cucumber strip out in a container and sprinkle salt over each strip. Layer the strips if necessary and refrigerate for 6 hours. After the 6 hours, wash the salt and liquid off the cucumber and fill each jar. Divide the mustard seeds, dill seeds and black pepper corns evenly among the jars. Bring the sugar and vinegar to a boil and fill each jar immediately. Shake any air bubbles to the top and refill till it overflows a bit. Tighten the lids and rinse under cold water to clean any sugar vinegar on glass. Store in a cool dark cupboard for 4 weeks and enjoy!

Yield: 2 small/medium jars I Recipe by Kim Sorensen

Danish Pickled Cucumber - Asier

Danish Pickled Cucumber- Agurksalat

In Denmark this is commonly served with pork, but I like it with anything... especially on hot dogs or at a Smorrebrod! You can make it a few hours before you need it and1or you can store it for months after you've opened it.

1 English cucumber	**15 peppercorns**
1 cup vinegar	**1 sprig Dill**
1 cup sugar	**1 medium size jar**

Sterilize your jar and lid in boiling hot water. Heat the vinegar and sugar in a pot... don't bring to a boil, just heat it till it's well dissolved and set aside to cool while you prepare your cucumber. Slice your cucumber in very thin slices (1mm). I use a slicer machine so all the slices are uniform. They should be thin enough so they can easily bend. Spread the cucumbers out on a cookie sheet and salt them generously. Let the cucumbers sit for 20 minutes to draw the water out. This makes the pickles crunchy. After 20 minutes rinse under cold water to remove the salt... then gently squeeze the water out and place into the jar. Place 15 peppercorns and a sprig of dill in the jar with the cucumber. Add the cooled sugar vinegar mixture into your jar. Put the lid on and shake gently to remove all the air bubbles to the top of the jar.

Yield: 1 medium size jar I Recipe by Kim Sorensen

Danish Pickled Cucumber- Agurksalat

Then remove the lid and fill with the remaining sugar vinegar mixture to the top of the jar. Put the lid on tight allowing any excess liquid to spill out. Tighten lid and rinse under cold water to clean the outside of the jar before storing in the fridge for a few hours before using.

Sides

Browned (Candied) Potatoes - Brunede Kartofler

This is a very traditional accompaniment to duck and pork dishes especially at Christmas. Tip #1: Heavily salt the water when boiling the potatoes. Tip #2: Be patient and let the butter sugar mixture turn deep brown colour before adding the potatoes.

30 parboiled and peeled　　　**4 tbsp (1/4 cup) butter**

very small potatoes　　　　　**6 tbsp (1/3 cup) white sugar**

In a fry pan at medium high heat, melt the butter. When the butter is hot, add the sugar and stir. Be patient and the mixture will eventually turn deep brown. After the butter and sugar mixture just turns a deep brown, add the potatoes and stir constantly.

Make sure to turn each potato over to coat both sides. When the potatoes are brown and well covered, sprinkle a little salt over the potatoes and serve immediately.

Yield: serves 6 - 8 persons I Recipe by Alfred's recipe

Browned Potatoes - Brunede Kartofler

Danish Red Cabbage - Rodkal

You can buy rodkaal in some European Deli stores but it's never as good as homemade. Once you peel your outer leaves off and cut out the stem out from the 1000 g red cabbage, you should be left with approximately 850 g. If you can't get red current jelly, you can use another cup of sugar, totalling 2 cups of sugar.

850 g red cabbage (stem removed and chopped into 1/2" squares)
2 cups vinegar

1 cup sugar
1 cup red current jelly 1 tsp salt

Bring 2 cups of vinegar and 1 cup of sugar to a gentle boil. Add the chopped cabbage and slow boil for one hour. Then mix in 1 cup of red current jelly and continue to boil for 10 minutes more or until the red cabbage is cooked but not too soft. Serve it immediately or put it in freezer bag(s) and freeze for use on another day.

Recipe by Kim Sorensen

Danish Red Cabbage - Rodkaal

Italian Salad - Italiensk salat

Italian Salad - Italiensk salat

Italian Salad is generally known as the topping for an open faced ham sandwich, but my northern family use it with almost everything and can sometimes be seen eating it alone by the bowlful. Yes, its that good! For the perfect Danish Italian Salad, don't overcook the macaroni, peas, carrots or asparagus. Make sure that all the macaroni, carrots, peas, corn and asparagus are cooked, thawed and DRY. If you don't want to use macaroni, then use a 112 cup instead of 113 cup of peas, carrots and asparagus. My mom makes this with Miracle Whip instead of mayonnaise. Some Danes even add a bit of mustard, sour cream.

1/4 cup cooked small elbow macaroni

1/3 cup cooked baby peas

1/3 cup cooked diced carrots

1/3 cup cooked sliced (1/4") thin asparagus

1/2 cup (113 g) mayonnaise Salt and pepper to taste

Combine in a bowl, the mayonnaise, macaroni, baby peas, diced carrots and chopped asparagus. Make sure to cool all the ingredients before mixing with the mayonnaise. Mix well and season with salt and pepper. For your open faced ham sandwich, place some arugula or other salad greens on buttered rye bread, then a generous portion of thin sliced ham and top with a huge dollop of Italian Salad and garnish with chives and a sprig of parsley or dill.

Yield: Yields 5 sandwiches I Recipe by Kim Sorensen

White sauce with peas and carrots - Hvid sause med rerter og gulerodder

This should be a very thick creamy seasoned white sauce with peas and carrots... a very traditional accompaniment to Karbonader. You can use a lighter milk, but the sweet creamy recipe attached is the best.

1 tbsp butter

2 tbsp of all-purpose flour

1/2 cup 3.25% milk

1/2 cup whipping cream

1/4 tsp sugar 1/4 salt

1/4 white pepper

2 cups peas and diced carrots

Melt butter in a pot. Mix the flour in the melted butter and cook for 30 sec. Whisk in the milk and cream very slowly if it is cold. Add the salt, pepper and sugar. Add the peas and carrots.

Recipe by Kim Sorensen

Danish Creamed Cabbage - Stuvet Hvidkal

This family favourite is easy to make. Tip #1, don't use too much water to boil the cabbage and then use all of the water in the sauce. This intensifies the cabbage flavour. Tip #2, Don't overcook the cabbage or it tastes mushy... the cabbage should be a bit more than al dente. Tip #3, you can add a little water right before serving if it is too thick, but remember you want this to be very creamy, not runny!

900 g (1 3/4 lbs) white cabbage chopped, stem removed

57 g (1/4 cup) butter

80 g (1/2 cup) all-purpose flour 350 g (1 1/2 cup) water

375g (1 1/2 cup) milk

240 g (1 cup) of heavy cream 1 tsp salt

1 tsp white pepper

Boil in a covered pot, the cabbage in 1 1/2 cups of water until al dente (do not overcook). Using a colander, drain the cabbage and reserve the water for the sauce. Make a roux with the butter and flour over medium heat in a sauce pan. Slowly whisk in all the reserved cabbage water that is left (should be about 1 cup) and then the milk and cream until the sauce thickens. Once your sauce is the right consistency (reasonably thick) add the salt and pepper. Add the cabbage, simmer for a couple of minutes and serve.

Yield: serves 8 - 10 I Recipe by Kim Sorensen

Danish Browned White Cabbage - Brunkaal

This was a favourite of Alfred's and very popular in Denmark. Many Danes love to add very meaty and thick Bacon pieces and some like to add caraway seeds.

500 g chopped White Cabbage 2 tbsp sugar

2 tbsp butter 1/8 tsp salt 1/4 cup of chicken broth

Place the butter in a large pot at medium high heat. When the butter is hot, add the sugar and spread it evenly. When the mixture is hot and turns brown, add the cabbage and stir to coat the cabbage. Don't add the cabbage until the sugar has turned brown. Add the salt and the broth. Cover and let simmer on low heat for an hour and serve.

Yield: Yields 4 person I Recipe by Kim Sorensen

Creamed Kale - Gronlangkal

This is a rich flavoured kale sauce that goes great with everything. For a richer sauce, use heavy cream.

454 g (1 lb) Kale 2 tbsp of butter 2 tbsp of flour

1/2 cup of hot milk

salt and pepper to taste 1 tsp sugar

1/8 tsp of nutmeg

Boil the kale in a covered medium size pot with a cup of lightly salted water for about 10 minutes. Remove the kale reserving the water. Remove the centre stem and chop the Kale fine. Heat the butter in the medium sized pot before adding the flour. Stir for a minute and slowly add the hot milk and then the reserved water. If the sauce is too thick, you need to add milk or kale juice. If it is too thin, boil a little more. Add the chopped kale, the sugar and nutmeg and then seasoning with salt and pepper to taste. Pour mixture into a blender and on the lowest setting, blend for 30 seconds. You want a coarse blend. Then put the mixture back into the pot and simmer for 5 minutes. The kale should be tender and ready to serve.

Yield: serves 4 I Recipe by Kim Sorensen

Creamed Kale - Grønlangkål

Cauliflower Casserole Dish - Blomkalsgratin

This is old Farfar's recipe except for the optional cheese and nutmeg. Even without the cheese and nutmeg this was a great family favourite side dish.

680 g (1 1/2 lb)
Cauliflower 1/2 cup flour
1/2 cup butter
1 cup warm milk
1 cup heavy
cream 5 eggs,
separated

2 tsp sugar
1 tsp salt
1 tsp pepper
1/4 tsp nutmeg (optional) 40 g
Gruyere finely grated (optional)
40 g Parmesan finely grated
(optional)

The sauce... Start by making a roux, melting the butter in a large sauce pan over medium heat. Add the flour and whisking until the all the butter and flour are combined. Slowly add in the warm milk, whisking constantly and then continue whisking in the cream.

You should have a very thick white sauce. Allow this to cool slightly, before mixing in the egg yolk. Add the salt and pepper before lastly adding the sugar. Beat the egg whites until they form stiff peaks and fold into the sauce mixture. The sauce should be very thick.

Yield: Serves 10 I Recipe by Alfred Sorensen

Cauliflower Casserole Dish - Blomkalsgratin

In a greased 9" x 9" baking dish, arrange the cauliflower in a single layer. Then pour the sauce over the cauliflower. Sprinkle the Gruyere and Parmesan on top. Bake at 350 degrees for 40 min until the cauliflower is baked through. Serve hot.

Bread

Danish Rye Bread - Rugbrod

This is the original Black Diamond Bakery recipe made by George Nielsen. Virtually, every Dane for two hundred of mile radius from Calgary has eaten this rye bread exclusively since the 1970's.

730 g Rogers Dark Rye Flour 730 g Arden Mills All-O-Wheat course whole wheat flour

30 g Salt

7 g Calcium Propionate

14 g Sour Dry Diorama

14 g Instant Dry Yeast (3x if using fresh yeast)

20 g Single Strength Carmel Liquid (or Molasses)

1000 g Lukewarm Water

Using a dough hook, mix well, all the ingredients in your mixer for up to 5 min. Then remove the dough to your flour dusted counter top. Roll by hand, the dough into an even 16" length roll and place in your pan and push the dough into the corners and flatten the top. Proof at 100 F for 2 hours or until the dough has risen to almost the top of the 4" pan. Then cover and bake at 360 F for 1 hour and 10 minutes. Remove from the oven and lightly cover with a towel and let cool on kitchen counter for a few hours then place in a plastic bag and store in the fridge overnight. Use the electric slicer in the morning when your loaf is cold.
Your slices should be 7 - 8 mm wide.

Yield: Yields one-16 x 4 x 4 or two-8 x 4 x 4 Bread Pan I Recipe by George Nielsen

Gramma's Legendary Rye Bread

This was the legendary ,Brown Bread, known around the Central Alberta Danish communities of Dickson, Kieversville, Raven and Spruceview.
Unfortunately, grandma never wrote down her recipes. Between my mom, Doris, her sister Dagney and myself, this is what we remember on how she made it. This recipe has been fine tuned to reflect everyone's thoughts and is as close as we're going to come up with. My mom remembers grandma needing the lard in by hand and using potato water, including little bits of potato mash instead of tap water. Hmmm...all I know is that her bread was legendary!

5 1/4 cups (835 g) Course Whole Wheat Bread Flour

3 cups (440 g) Light Rye Flour

4.6 tsp (32 g) salt

1 1/2 Pkge, 3 tsp (15 g) of Active Yeast

1/4 cup (92 g) molasses

8 tsp (35 g) packed brown sugar 1/3 cup (70 g) melted lard

3 1/3 cups (750 g) warm (35 C) water

Place the flour and yeast in a mixing bowl. Mix and dissolve well the warm water, molasses, brown sugar, melted lard and salt and add to the mixing bowl.

Using a dough hook, mix well for up to 5 minutes or until very well mixed. The dough (2,256 g) should be easy to handle. Using a little flour on your counter and hands roll the dough out by hand into a 1 - 16" roll or 2 - 8" rolls (1,128 g each) and place in your pan(s) and press evenly into the corners, and before proofing it in a damp oven at 100 C for 1 to 2 hours.

Yield: One 16 or 2 - 8 x 4 x 4 inch loaf pans I Recipe by Kim Sorensen

Gramma's Legendary Rye Bread

When the dough rises to about an inch below the top of your pan, you're ready to put it in the oven. Bake at 360 for 1 hr and 10 min in your pan. Wipe a little butter on the top, cover with a cloth and cool on counter before bagging and refrigerating overnight.
In the morning slice the bread 9 mm, or as you prefer.

French White Bread - Franskbrod

You can make this bread in a bread pan or on a cookie sheet as is typically done for French Bread. If you use a cookie sheet, add a little more flour to make sure the dough is stiff. You want the dough to hold its shape.

2 1/2 cups (600 g) warm water 2 tbsp (24 g) instant yeast

6 cups (1000 g) bread flour

3.5 tsp (30 g) salt

1/3 cup (80 g) vegetable oil 1/4 cup (55 g) sugar

1 egg beaten - for glazing bread

In your electric mixing bowl equipped with a dough hook, place all the ingredients and start to mix. When well mixed, remove dough and roll into a long roll.

Then place in your greased bread pan(s) (1 - 16" or 2 - 8") and let rise in your proofing oven (100 F) or a warm spot on your counter. After an hour, gently kneed the dough right in your pan(s), flattening the dough and pushing it into the corners. Let the dough rise again to about 3/4 of the height of your pan. Be aware that it will continue to rise a bit when baking, so you would want to start baking once it has risen to around the height of your pan. When you're ready to start baking, cut at an angle the top of your loaf and then brush the top of your loaf with your beaten egg. Place on the middle rack for 30 minutes at 375. The top should be dark golden brown.

Yield: one 16 or two 8 x 4 x 4 inch loaves I Recipe by Kim Sorensen

French White Bread - Franskbrod

When done, remove from the pans and rub a little butter on top and let cool on the counter. Once the bread has cooled enough, bag it and place in the fridge overnight. In the morning, slice your bread 12 mm.

Kim's Whole Wheat Bread with seeds

This is a very tasty whole wheat bread with seeds and rolled oats. I like to use ,coarse, whole wheat flour with the all purpose white flour, rolled oats and seeds for that grainy texture. You can substitute the seeds for any combination of sesame, pine, flax, poppy, pumpkin, caraway, sunflower and1or chia seeds. I like the ones with sesame, sunflower or pine seeds with the rolled oats topping.

490 g (2 3/4 cups) whole wheat flour

300 g (1 3/4 cups) all purpose flour

410 g (1 3/4 cups) warm water 7 g (2 1/4 tsp) instant yeast

37 g (3 tbsp) brown sugar

43 g (3 tbsp) soften butter

11 g (1 1/2 tsp) salt

100 g (3/4 cup) sesame, sunflower and pine seeds 1 egg whisked

1/4 cup rolled oats

Pour warm water into your mixing bowl and add the yeast. Let the yeast wake up for a few minutes and is frothing before adding all the other ingredients. Then using your mixer and a dough fork, mix everything for 5 - 10 minutes. The sides of the bowl should be clean and the dough should be slightly sticky to touch. With your board and your hands floured, remove the dough and place on the board. Roll the dough into a nice 10" x 6" roll and place into your bread pan coated with pam or olive oil. Place into the proofing oven or leave in a warm place like the top of the fridge until it has doubled in size. Then kneed the dough while still in the bread pan and let rise again.

Yield: 1 - 10 x 6 loaf I Recipe by Kim Sorensen

Kim's Whole Wheat Bread with seeds

Then remove the dough to your board and kneed it for a minute or two. Roll it into a smooth 10" x 6" roll and place back into the bread pan. Let rise again until it has risen well past the pan sides. Brush plenty of egg wash on top of the loaf. Sprinkle and pat down plenty of rolled oats on top. Now place in the bottom rung of the oven set at 350 F for 45 minutes or until the internal temperature is between 195 - 200 F. Remove from the oven and cool completely before slicing.

Breakfast

Danish Pancake Balls - !Ebleskiver

Very popular Danish treat especially with the kids, Serve ./Ebleskiverr as a treat, dessert or anytime special. The trick to making the perfect aebleskiver is to have the batter not runny, but not too thick. When you turn the aebleskiver the top should flow to the bottom of the pan making the perfect round ./Ebleskiver. You should only turn them once golden brown. Use a fork, pointed small spoon or a pointed chop stick to turn the aebleskiver.

2 cups all purpose flour 2 eggs separated

1/4 tsp salt

2 tsp baking powder

1/2 tsp baking soda 2 tsp of vanilla

2 cups buttermilk

1/4 cup melted butter 2 tbsp sugar

Separate the eggs putting the yolks in a mixing bowl and whites in a very clean mixmaster bowl and beat until light and fluffy, then set aside. In the mixing bowl with the yolks, add the flour, salt, baking powder, baking soda, vanilla buttermilk, butter and sugar and mix until smooth. Make sure you have the right texture before gently folding in the egg whites. Add some oil or butter to each of the holes in the aebleskiver pan before adding some of the batter. Fill the holes about 3/4 from bottom and using a fork, turn once they are brown and top still soft. Do not burn them. Slit a hole in the side with a sharp pointy knife and fill with whipping cream, honey, cheese or jam. Sprinkle with icing sugar and serve.

Yield: Makes approximately 45-50 JEbleskiver I Recipe by Kim Sorensen

Danish Pancake Balls - Aebleskiver

Danish Hash - Biksemad

Danish Hash - Biksemad

Historically, this breakfast is made from yesterday's leftovers. The original Biksemad was simply potatoes, onions and leftover meat with an egg or two on top. Today, their are many versions... this is mine.

1 or 2 fried eggs per person 300 g cooked and cubed potatoes 375 g pork sausage meat

1 medium onion diced 300 g of vegetables diced (zucchini, carrots, asparagus, peppers and mushrooms) Oil, butter or grease to fry Salt and pepper to season

In a fry pan, fry the pork sausage till it's no longer pink and reserve meat in a bowl. Pour out most of the grease. Saute the potatoes in the fry pan (add butter if needed) until golden brown and also reserve in the meat bowl. Now saute the onions until caramelized then add all the vegetables together and cook until just el dente. Add the meat and potatoes and simmer (fry) till everything is hot. Season with salt and pepper. Place a dollop of the mixture in the middle of each plate and then place the fried egg(s) on top.

Sprinkle a bit of chopped green onions around for garnish and enjoy one of my favourite breakfasts!

Yield: Yields 8 persons I Recipe by Kim Sorensen

Danish Yogurt - Tykmrelk

Farfar enjoyed this yogurt breakfast once a week. When ever I buy buttermilk I always make myself this yogurt breakfast. I use a sugar syrup or maple syrup but you also use some brown sugar... you can use anything sweet, even fruit. I like to make this Yogurt right at supper time because then its perfect timing to have for breakfast in 36 hours.

1 cup of whole milk

1 tbsp of

Buttermilk

1/4 cup of rye bread crumbs

1/4 cup of sugar syrup

Pour the whole milk in a small soup bowl and add 1 tbsp of buttermilk. Stir and then leave covered in a warm place like the top of the fridge for 36 hours to set. Old Farfar would add rye bread crumbs and syrup.

Yield: 1 serving I Recipe by Farfar

Danish Rice Porridge - Risengrod

Breakfast or dessert... your choice! This is a very filling dish, so serve in small amounts.

1 cup short-grained glutinous rice (such as jasmine or pearl) 1 tsp butter

2 tsp sugar 1/2 tsp salt 5 cups milk
Cinnamon-sugar and butter to taste

Place in a heavy bottom pot, the rice, milk, sugar, salt and butter and slow boil (1 - 2 hours) till the liquid is absorbed into the rice. The rice should be soft, creamy and slightly sweet. Place in a serving bowl, place a small amount of the rice mixture, a small dollop of butter in the middle of the rice and sprinkle liberal amounts of the cinnamon and sugar mixture throughout.

Yield: 6 servings I Recipe by Kim Sorensen

Danish Rye Bread Porridge - Ollebrod

Farfar made this for us kids many a mornings. It's delicious! Use all water and no beer if you want. The beer I used in this recipe is Carlsberg or Tuborg.

200 g (3 C) Danish rye bread

350 g (1 1/2C) water

58 g (1/4 C) regular

beer 77 g (1/3 C)

white sugar

1 C heavy Cream

2 tbsp white sugar

1/2 tsp of Vanilla

extract 4 dollops of

butter

First, whip the heavy cream, sugar and vanilla extract until stiff and set aside. Break the rye bread into small pieces and place in a pot with the beer, water and sugar. Using moderate heat, whisk the porridge until smooth. Once the porridge has reached a boil, remove and pour equal portions into 4 bowls. Place a dollop of butter into a well in the middle of the porridge and top with a dollop of whipped whipping cream and serve.

Yield: 4 servings I Recipe by Kim Sorensen

Salads

Grilled Caesar Salad

This isn't exactly Danish, but it's been a hit at many dinner parties for many years. Found this recipe at Grilled Expeditions in Phoenix.

1 large head of Romaine Lettuce

3-6 cloves of Garlic sliced thin

2 large egg (boiled 1 1/2 min)

2 tsp of Dijon Mustard

2 tsp of Worcestershire Sauce

1 1/2 cup (85 g) packed finely grated Parmigiana Reggiano

2 tbsp (35 g) lemon juice 2 tbsp of mayonnaise

1 tin (25 g) Anchovies Fillets chopped

1/3 cup of Olive Oil 1 tsp pepper

1/4 tsp of salt or to taste

3 strips fried crispy bacon cut in 1" lengths

DRESSING (Can be done a day ahead of time) -Using a fork, mash the sliced garlic in the bottom of a large size bowl. Now whisk in, the egg, dijon mustard, Worcestershire sauce, Parmigiana Reggiano cheese, lemon juice, mayonnaise, anchovies, olive oil, salt and pepper. Refrigerate until ready to use............................ GRILLING THE ROMAINE. Discard any bruised or wilted outer leafs. Trim about 1/2" off the discoloured stem end. Trim some of the top of the romaine head if it is longer than the plate it is to be served on. Cut Romaine lengthwise in 4 quarters.

Yield: Yields 4 servings I Recipe by Kim Sorensen found at Grilled Expeditions in Phoenix

Grilled Ceasar Salad

Brush the quarters with olive oil and grill on a hot barbecue for 1 minute or less on both sides... the outside should be just slightly wilted, maybe even dark tinges of the edges and still crisp on the inside. PLATING. Place each quarter of romaine on a plate and spoon plenty of dressing on the romaine. Garnish with a large slice of Parmigiana Reggiano cheese and a few small bacon slices and serve.

Emmy's Honey Curry Spinach Salad

Dressing

1/2 onion chopped 1 tsp paprika

1 tsp curry powder

1/2 tsp mustard powder or

1 tsp Dijon mustard

1/2 tsp turmeric 1/2 tsp celery seeds

1/2 tsp salt

1/3 cup cider vinegar 1/2 cup honey

1 cup safflower oil Salad

1 bag spinach leaves

1/2 cup toasted almonds 1/2 cup red onions sliced

1 orange peeled and sliced

In blender, combine onion, paprika, curry powder, mustard, turmeric, celery seeds and salt. Blend well and then add the vinegar and honey. In a steady stream finish with safflower oil. Toss salad with just enough of the dressing to coat the spinach. You will have dressing left over for a few more salads! You can toast the almonds in the oven or in a skillet until they just start to turn brown.

Recipe by Shelley Adams from the Whitewater Cooks

Wilted Spinach Salad

I like to slice the bacon lengthwise into three long pieces and then cut them crosswise in 112, pieces before frying. This recipe can be made up to a day in advance and stored in the refrigerator.

1 garlic clove chopped fine

2 tbsp cider or red wine vinegar 1 tsp sugar

1 tsp salt

1 tsp dry mustard 1/2 tsp pepper

6 tbsp salad oil

1 cup T-sliced mushrooms 1 cup T-sliced cauliflower

8 cups spinach Stems removed 3 hard boiled eggs grated

8 slices bacon diced large reserved bacon drippings

3 green onions, chopped fine

In a covered container, mix together the first 7 ingredients. In a fry pan, fry the bacon and add the bacon to the covered container reserving the bacon grease in the pan to be used later. Store the covered container in the refrigerator until ready to use. In a large bowl, add the spinach, eggs, bacon, green onions, mushrooms and cauliflower. Both containers can be stored in the refrigerator for up to a day in advance. When ready to serve, heat the pan with the reserved bacon grease and add the all the contents of the covered container. Heat for 1-2 minutes. Now add the hot dressing to the large bowl, toss well and serve immediately.

Yield: 6-8 serving I Recipe by Best of Bridge

Broccoli, Mushroom, Raisin Salad with Sweet and Sour Dressing

Dressing

1 large egg

1 large egg yolk

1/2 cup sugar

1/2 tsp dry mustard

1 1/2 tsp cornstarch

1/4 cup white vinegar 1/4 cup water

1/4 tsp salt

2 tbsp soft butter cut into bits 1/2 cup mayonnaise

Salad

4 cups blanched small broccoli flowerets

1 cup raisins

1 cup sliced mushrooms 1/4 cup chopped red onion

6 sliced crumbled fried bacon

DRESSING. In a small Bowl, whisk together the egg, egg yolk, sugar, mustard and cornstarch. In a saucepan combine and bring to a boil using moderate heat, the vinegar, water and salt. Whisk in the egg mixture and cook while whisking for 1 minute or until it has thickened. Remove pan from heat and whisk in the butter. Then whisk in the mayonnaise and chill the dressing covered in the refrigerator. SALAD. In a large bowl gently combine the broccoli, rasins, mushrooms, onions and bacon. Pour the salad dressing over the salad and toss well. Add salt and pepper to taste.

Yield: Serves 6.

Mandarin Almond Salad

1 head lettuce shredded

6 green onions

1 tin mandarin oranges
chopped

1/2 cup almond pieces

2 tsp water

2 tbsp white sugar

1 tsp margarine or soft butter

Dressing

1/3 cup salad oil

3 tbsp white vinegar 3 tbsp white
sugar 3/4 tsp salt

pepper to taste

Heat the almond pieces, water, white sugar and margarine in microwave and stir until well coated and browned (approx 2 1/2 min) Set aside so mixtures cools. For the dressing and in a small bowl, mix well the salad oil, vinegar, white sugar, salt and pepper. In a large bowl, toss well the lettuce, green onions and the salad dressing. Add the mandarin oranges and almond pieces mixture on top as garnish.

Yield: Serves 6 - 8 persons I Recipe by Best of Bridge

Sauces

Danish Tartar Sauce - Remoulade (most common and sweet)

There are many recipes for Remoulade. You can easily buy this type of Danish Remoulade in many Deli stores. I definitely recommend making your own, but there's nothing wrong with buying the remoulade.

1 kg green tomatoes 1	**530 ml (2.11 cups) vinegar**
1/2 kg zucchini 600 g	**750 g sugar**
onions	**40 g dry mustard 3 tsp mild curry**
60 ml (1/4 cup) of salt	**150 ml (.63 cups) flour**

Make sure all vegetables are chopped very fine. Then in a large bowl, mix the salt and the vegetables and let stand for 1 hour. Put the vegetables into a large thin cotton t-towel and squeeze all the water out. Put into a large pot with 1/2 litre of water and 200 ml of the vinegar. Boil for 20 minutes. Stir well so it does not burn. When it has cooled down, squeeze the liquid out again using your large t-towel. Now put the mixture back into the pot and add 330 ml vinegar, sugar, mustard powder and curry. Let it boil, stirring well. Mix the flour with a little water, so it is not lumpy. Use a blender or food processor if you prefer. Then add the flour mixture to your pot of vegetables and stir. Reduce the heat and let simmer for 20 minutes before putting it into your canning jars. When ready, mix 50/50 with mayo and serve.

Yield: makes 12 x 125 ml jars I Recipe by Kathy Sorensen

Danish Tartar sauce - Remoulade

This is a unique remoulade that is not sweet and is especially great on hot dogs. Make sure to dice the ingredients FINE or use a food processor. Remoulade is used for a variety of Danish dishes and sandwiches.

3 tbsp (50 g) mayonnaise

1 tbsp (18 g) sour cream

1 tbsp (10 g) carrots, (diced fine)

1 tbsp (12 g) capers (chopped)

1 tbsp (12 g) red cabbage (diced fine)

1 tbsp (15 g) Dill Pickle (diced fine)

1 tbsp (15 g) Sweet Bread and Butter Pickle (diced fine)

1 tbsp (6 g) Chives (diced fine) 1 tsp (5 g) Shallot (diced fine) 1 tbsp (15 g) Lemon Juice

1 tsp (7 g) strong Mustard

1 tsp (3 g) Turmeric

2 tsp (12 g) sugar 1/2 tsp (4 g) salt Pepper to taste

Mix all ingredients together and refrigerate for an hour before serving.

Yield: serves 4 I Recipe by Kim Sorensen

Kim's Curry Sauce

This is a great sauce I use for some Danish Open Face Sandwiches.

2 tbsp mayonnaise 1
tbsp sour cream
1 tsp curry powder

1/4 tsp lemon juice 1/4 tsp
garlic powder 1/8 tsp sugar
pinch of cayenne

Mix all ingredients in a bowl and refrigerate at least 1/2 hour or until needed. You can make this days ahead of time.

Yield: 4 small toppings I Recipe by Kim Sorensen

Kim's Caviar and Onion Sauce

I use this sauce for some seafood sandwiches.

2 tbsp mayonnaise 1
tbsp sour cream
3/4 tsp onion powder

2 tsp black caviar 1/2 tsp
lemon juice 1/4 tsp sugar

Mix all ingredients together and refrigerate for 1/2 hour or until needed. Can be made a day in advance.

Yield: 4 small toppings I Recipe by Kim Sorensen

Kim's Blue Cheese Sauce

If you love blue cheese, then you'll love this rich creamy blue cheese sauce. You can use this sauce on anything, even Danish sandwiches, but I love this as a salad dressing on a wedge of iceberg lettuce, sliced Bosc pear, candied pecans and bacon bits. Tip... The crumbled blue cheese usually comes in 4 oz containers. This recipe calls for 2 containers using 6 oz. Use the last 2 oz of crumbled blue cheese as a garnish for an even more blue cheesy taste!

6 oz blue cheese crumbled

1 1/2 cups mayonnaise

1/4 cup sour cream 2 tbsp buttermilk

1 1/2 tsp white wine vinegar

1 tsp Worcestershire sause

1/2 tsp mustard powder 1/2 tsp garlic powder

1/2 tsp sugar 1/4 tsp salt

1/4 tsp pepper

Using a fork, lightly mash the crumbled blue cheese with the mayonnaise in a bowl... don't mash too much as you want to end with a lumpy mixture. Then whisk and combine the remaining ingredients and refrigerate.

Yield: 8 servings I Recipe by Kim Sorensen

Dijon Mustard Tarragon Sauce

This is a great sauce to use with fillet mignon steaks.

3 cups chicken stock 2 cups dry sherry

2 cups heavy cream

1/3 cup dijon mustard

1/2 cup fresh tarragon leaves salt and pepper to taste

Bring the sherry to a boil in a deep pan and add the chicken stock. Reduce the liquid for about 10 minutes, then add the cream, dijon mustard, tarragon and salt and pepper to taste. Reduce the sauce to a liquid syrupy consistency.

Yield: 4 portions I Recipe by Paul Owens from The Cliff in Barbados

Danish Soups

Chicken Broth - Kyllingefond

You can buy chicken broth from the grocery store, but if you want the best broth, you have to buy a whole chicken and make your own. Nothing is wasted, even the chicken meat is used in the Danish creamy Chicken and Asparagus Tarteletter (,huns i asparges,). Tip #1, If you slow boil with a good fitting lid, you will not loose very much liquid. I often will end up with the same or close to the same amount of liquid I put in at the start. Tip #2, if you want a sweeter broth add a parsnip. If you want a clearer broth, don't boil with carrots. For a nice aroma, add some thyme. For a stronger and more flavourful broth use 12 to 14 cups of water.

**1 whole chicken 16
cups of water
2 celery sticks cut up**

**1 large onion quartered
1 handful of fresh parsley 6 Bay leafs
Salt to taste**

Rinse your chicken under cold water and place in a large pot with 16 cups of water as this should be more than enough to cover the chicken. Then add all other ingredients and slow boil with the lid on for 4 hours. Remove from heat and allow to cool a bit. Then using a colander pour the broth into a large pot. Once the remaining chicken has cool enough, remove all the chicken meat to a container to be place in the fridge for use later. Discard all remaining skin, bones and vegetables. Pour the broth (15 to 16 cups) one more time through a cloth strainer and back into the original but rinsed out pot.

Yield: 15 to 16 cups I Recipe by Kim Sorensen

Chicken Broth - Kyllingefond

Heat the broth and season with salt. Then store the pot of broth in the fridge overnight. In the morning remove any hardened fat on top of the broth. The remaining liquid is now a premium chicken broth that can be used in soups, gravies and many other recipes. Use the broth now or freeze it in a container for use later.

Danish Chicken Soup - Dansk Kyllingesuppe

Danish chicken soup is made with a flavourful, clear chicken broth, vegetables such as carrots, parsnips and leeks, small-sized pork or beef meatballs, and dumplings can all be made ahead of time. Do not boil the meat balls, dumplings, carrots, parsnips or leeks in the broth as this will discolour the broth making it murky instead of the intended clear broth. Have the vegetables cooked and ready to put in the hot soup. I like to steam instead of boiling the carrots, parsnips and leeks, thus preserving their nutritional value, colour and taste. Soup should be served hot, so warm up the bowls and slow simmer the carrots, parsnips, leeks, meat balls and white dumplings in the soup just before you're ready to serve. For an every day hearty soup for the family, serve it with plenty of carrots, parsnips, leeks, meat balls and dumplings. For a dinner party, serve the soup as a course with only a few of each for a more sophisticated gourmet look that puts the emphasis on the soup's broth (Clear Soup)... and make no mistake, this soup is all about the broth!

10 cups Chicken Broth

2 cups Carrots cooked sliced 2 cups Parsnips cooked sliced

1 cup Leeks cooked sliced

2 cups Soup Meat Balls 2 cups Soup Dumplings

Heat the broth to a slow boil. Using the oven, warm 10 large flat soup bowls, carrots, parsnips, leeks, meat balls and dumplings. Now add 1 - 2 cup of hot broth to each soup bowl with the preferred amount of carrots, parsnips, leeks, meat balls and white dumplings to each bowl. Garnish with a sprig of parsley and serve hot.

Yield: 10 large bowls I Recipe by Kim Sorensen

125

Danish Chicken Soup, called "Danish Clear Soup", has meat balls, white dumplings, carrots, and parsnips.

Meat Balls for Soup - Kodkugler til Suppe

You can use any combination of pork or beef.

3/4 tsp Salt

225 g (8 oz) ground
pork 1/2 tsp white
pepper

1 egg

2 tbsp chopped fresh parsley 1/4
cup of chicken stock

1/3 cup all purpose flour

Mix together the pork, salt, the white pepper, egg, 1/3 cup of flour and 1/4 cup of the chicken stock in a bowl until well combined. Using a small spoon and cold water, dip the spoon in between each meatball so the mixture does not stick to your hand or the spoon.

Scoop some of the meatball mixture with the spoon and roll into a tiny meat ball using the palm of your hand and the teaspoon. Cook small batches in a pot of boiling water for 4 to 5 minutes, then remove with a slotted spoon and let cool completely. Continue with small batches until the remaining meatball mixture is gone.

Yield: 40 small meat balls (enough for 8 to 10 bowls of soup I Recipe by Kim Sorensen

White Dumplings for soup -Melboller, til suppe

These white dumplings are used in Danish soups like Danish Clear Soup.

78 g (1/2 cup) Flour

50 g (1/4 cup) butter 2 whole large eggs

120 g (1/2 cup) of water 1/4 tsp salt

1/4 tsp white pepper

a pinch of cardamon (optional)

On low heat, melt the butter in a pan, then add water, salt, pepper and finally the flour. Mash well and remove from heat to cool down, then when the dough is just cool enough, add the egg and mix well. Your dough should be thick paste like, shiny, but not runny. Heat a pot of salted water with a little vegetable oil to almost boiling (DO NOT BOIL). Using a danish bollesprotje, a cookie press or something similar or just use a plastic zip lock bag and cut a 1.5 cm section off the corner and press the dough through and using a knife to cut 1.5 cm pieces into the almost boiling salty water. Do them in 2 or 3 batches so you don't leave the first ones in cooking too long.

As soon as the dumplings rise to the top, use a slotted spoon and immediately put into a bowl of ice cold water and then immediately into a container to store in the fridge. You can make these dumplings well ahead of time.

Yield: Serves 10 I Recipe by Kim Sorensen

DANISH YELLOW SPLIT PEA SOUP
- Gule !Erter

This is a very hearty Danish soup! Great for a quick reheat supper on a cold winters day!
Tip: In Denmark, they use Vienna sausages which are hard to find over here, so you can use
a thin, small, mild, but great tasting sausage of your choice instead, but not wieners!

2 cups (450 g) yellow split
peas 8 cups (1,850 g) water

1 tsp salt

1 tsp pepper

125 gm Vienna sausages,
chopped

500 g meaty bacon, chopped

1 (6-900 g) smoked ham hock

2 (130g) stalks celery, chopped

3 (260g) leek stems, chopped 3 (200 g)
carrots, peeled & chopped

2 (300 g) potatoes, peeled & chopped

1 (200 g) onion, chopped

Heat the water, ham hock and yellow split peas in a large
covered pot. Once it is boiling, lower heat to a slow boil for 1
hour. Fry the bacon in a large fry pan till most of the fat is
rendered out and bacon pieces are not crisp. Add the bacon to
the pot leaving as much of the rendered fat. Add the rest of the
ingredients, celery, carrots, leeks, onions, potatoes, Vienna
sausages, salt and pepper into the large pot and simmer for at
least 1 more hour or until the yellow split peas have mushed.

Yield: Serves 6 - 8 I Recipe by Kim Sorensen

DANISH YELLOW SPLIT PEA SOUP
-Gule !Erter

Remove the hock from the soup and remove the meat leaving the bone, skin and fat to discard. Chop the meat into small pieces and put back into soup. It's very Danish to serve buttered rye bread, a good mustard, and pickled beets with this soup.

Cold Buttermilk Soup - Koldskal

This is a family favourite. Served on hot days or anytime as a treat. My family often just drank this right out of a glass. Yummy!

4 egg

4 cups buttermilk 3/4

cup sugar

1 teaspoon vanilla extract

Graham cracker crumbs

1 tsp lemon zest (optional)

Beat egg yolks and sugar until lemony colour. Then add the vanilla and whisk in buttermilk slowly. Ladle into a bowl and sprinkle with lots of graham cracker crumbs on top and serve cold.

Yield: 6 servings I Recipe by Farfar and Doris's recipe

Hot Buttermilk soup - Krernemrelksuppe

A family favourite. Serve this anytime! It's even great cold the next day!

4 cups of buttermilk

1/2 cup of sugar

1 tsp vanilla extract

2 tsp potato starch 1/2 cup raisins

1 cup heavy cream

Heat the buttermilk, sugar, vanilla extract and raisins in a pot. Once at a low boil, add potato starch until it has thicken. Add the heavy cream at the end and ladle into bowls. Sprinkle with ground cinnamon and serve immediately.

Yield: serves 6 I Recipe by Kim Sorensen

Danish potato soup - Kartoffel Suppe

My Grandma used to make a version of this for me when I was just a little boy on their farm. She used whole milk instead of water and ham bone. Oh so good!

1 meaty ham bone Water

2 medium potatoes, peeled and diced

6 green onions, sliced 3 celery ribs, chopped

1/4 cup minced fresh parsley 2 cups chopped cabbage

2 medium carrots, diced

3 tablespoons all-purpose flour 1 cup half-and-half cream

Ground nutmeg

In a pot, bring the ham bone and 2 quarts water to a boil. Reduce heat and simmer 1 hour or until meat pulls away from the bone. Remove ham bone. When cool enough to handle, trim any meat and dice.

Discard bone. Return ham to kettle along with potatoes, onions, celery, parsley, cabbage and carrots; cook 40 minutes. Using a small container with a tight lid, shake vigorously the flour and 1/4 cup cold water until smooth. Slowly pour into the boiling soup, stirring constantly until the soup thickens. Cook the soup for 2 more minutes. Reduce heat; stir in cream. Remove from the heat. Garnish with nutmeg.

Yield: 6 large bowls I Recipe by Kim Sorensen

Danish Potato Soup - Kartoffel Suppe

Danish Open Face Sandwiches

All the following sandwiche pictures come from the Legendary Original Ida Davidson Restaurant in Copenhagn, Denmark

Danish Open Face Sandwiches - Smorrebrod

The following are a sample of some of the most favourite open face sandwiches. But note, the recognized queen of the open face sandwich is Ida Davidsen. She has the oldest running restaurant and her family is the ones that started the open face sandwiches in the late 1800's. She has had up to 250 different open face sandwiches! So what is listed here is only a sample. If you want to step out of your comfort zone and try something different, go to the Ida Davidsen smorrebrod website and view the latest creations from the queen of smorrebrod! Be creative and invent your own sandwich. If you're ever in Denmark, make sure to stop in at the Ida Davidsen Restaurant in the heart of Copenhagn for a must see visit!

Ham Sandwich

1 slice Danish rye bread
Butter
85 g (3 oz) thinly slice
ham 1 large butter lettuce
leaf

1 large dollop of "italian salad"
2 thinly sliced cucumber 2 cherry tomatoes halved
Diced parsley

On a buttered slice of Danish rye bread, place the large leaf of lettuce and then a liberal amount of thinly slice ham. On top, place a large dollop of italian salad. Garnish the top with cherry tomatoes, 2 thinly sliced cucumber and dices parsley.

Yield: 1 full sandwich

Warm Roast Pork Sandwich

1 slice of buttered Danish
rye bread
1 - 2 slices of warm roast
pork 1 dollop of warm
red cabbage

2 large pickled beets
2 thinly sliced cucumber
1/4 cup hot rich brown
gravy diced parsley

On the buttered Danish rye bread, place 1 or 2 slices of roast
pork. Place a dollop of pickled red cabbage and the pickled beets
on top. Garnish with the cucumbers and parsley. Serve warm with
the gravy on the side.

Yield: 1 full sandwich

Danish Liver Pate - Leverpostej

1 slice of buttered Danish
rye bread

2 slices of liver pate

10 slices of fried
mushrooms

1 strip of fried bacon

lingonberry jam or

pickled beets

a handful of deep fried
diced parsley

Place 2 slices of liver pate on the buttered Danish rye bread. Place a strip of fried bacon on top of the pate. Now crisscross the sandwich with a row of mushrooms, parsley and lingonberry jam. Substitute the jam with pickled beets if desired.

Yield: 1 full sandwich

Liver Pate - Leverpostej

This is a family favourite and quite possibly one of the most recognized open face sandwich at a Smorrebrod. This recipe uses pork lard instead of actual pork fat. Simply put, it's way easier to use a blender and lard than a meat grinder and pork fat. The end result is about the same. When you use a blender you will be making the Leverpostej fine in texture. If you want it coarser, use a meat grinder and grind the liver and pork fat once, twice or three times to get the texture you like best. You can freeze the Leverpostej raw in the containers and when ready, simply defrost and then bake as instructed. Cooked leverpostej does not freeze well.

500 g (1.1 lbs) pork liver cut into small pieces

300 g (4.4 lbs) pork lard

120 g (2) eggs

260 g onions roughly chopped 480 g (2 cups) hot milk

75 g (10 tbsp) all purpose flour

30 g (2 tbsp) butter 3/4 tsp pepper

1 1/2 tsp salt

1/2 tsp ground allspice 1/4 tsp ground cloves 4-5 5" strips of bacon

Using a fry pan, make a runny roux by melting the lard and then mixing in the flour. Stir for 1 minute, then slowly pour in the hot milk. Stir until well mixed. Then pour the roux in a blender. Using a blender at the lowest speed, mix the roux, eggs, onions, salt, pepper, allspice and cloves. Slowly add the liver and mix well. Pour the mixture into aluminum trays and place one strip of bacon on top. Set the trays into a pan of shallow hot water.

Yield: Makes 4 to 5 - 6" x 4" x 2" aluminum trays I Recipe by Kim Sorensen

Liver Pate - Leverpostej

Bake at 350 F (175 C) for 1 hr if using a small pan and up to 1 hr and 15 min if using a large pan. Either way the internal temperature should be 176 F (75 C). Cool in the fridge and you're ready to go! Serve on rye bread with pickled beets or red cabbage.

Beef Sandwich

1 slice of Danish rye
bread butter

1 quartered hard
boiled egg

crispy fried onions

3 thin slices tomatoes cold bearnaise
sauce

On a slice of buttered Danish Rye Bread place a liberal amount of roast beef. Down the middle put a liberal amount of cold bearnaise sauce. On top of the bearnaise sauce place 3 slices of tomatoes. A long each side of the tomatoes place 2 of the quartered eggs.
Place on top of the tomatoes a liberal amount of fried onions. Remoulade can be substituted for Bearnaise.

Yield: 1 full slice sandwich

Fillet of Plaice

1 slice buttered Danish
rye bread
1 large fried fillet of
Plaice 4-6 Shrimp
Remoulade

lemon wedge
cooked asparagus spears lux roll
caviar

Place the fish on the slice of buttered rye bread. Put a generous portion of remoulade down the centre of the fillet. Arrange the shrimp on top of the remoulade, finishing with the roll of lux filled with black caviar at the end. Garnish with the lemon wedge and asparagus spears.

Yield: 1 full sandwich

Shrimp and Egg

1 slice buttered white bread

1-2 hard boiled eggs quartered

20 small boiled shrimp

spicy mayonnaise

fresh dill sprigs

Place down the middle of the buttered white bread a healthy amount of spicy mayonnaise. Place a row of egg on either side of the mayonnaise and then two rows of shrimp on top in the middle. Garnish with dill sprigs.

Yield: 1 full sandwich

Lox and Scrambled Egg

1 slice of buttered white bread 85 g (3 0z) lox

2 eggs scrambled dill sprigs

Stack a generous portion of lox on top of the buttered white bread. Down the middle and the length of the sandwich, place a generous portion of scrambled eggs. Garnish with dill sprigs.

Yield: 1 full sandwich

Danish "Shooting Star" Open Face Sandwich - Stjerneskud

This is Denmark's National Sandwich and it is without a doubt, very decadent and delicious! Serve this if you want a wow factor! Tip #1 You can prepare some of the items a day ahead like both sauces, rolling up the fish to be steamed, rolling up the lox, boiling the eggs and washing the lettuce leaves. Tip #2 The key to a great ,Shooting Star Sandwich, is having the all the hot items ,hot, when assembling the sandwich. So start the frying of fillets, steaming of the fish, boiling the shrimps and steaming the asparagus, so that they all are completed close to the same time. Then the parts that are suppose to be warm, will be.

Yield: 4 Open Face Sandwiches I Recipe by Kim Sorensen

Danish "Shooting Star" Open Face Sandwich - Stjerneskud

4 plaice or sole fillets

FRIED LARGER FILLETS

salt and pepper for seasoning

1/4 cup all purpose flour

2 hardboiled eggs quartered

1/2 cup bread or panko crumbs butter or oil for frying **STEAMED SMALLER FILLETS**

1/2 cup white wine

2 cups very salty water **OTHER MEATS AND CONDIMENTS**

4 slices of smoked lox salmon 200 g (40/bag size) frozen uncooked peeled and deveined shrimp

a jar of black and red roe or caviar

1 glass of white asparagus

8 trimmed green asparagus 2 hard boiled eggs quartered

10-12 cherry tomatoes cut in half

8 large lettuce leaves

8 thinly sliced crosswise lemon slices

8 thinly sliced cucumber slices

jar of Danish remoulade

4 large sprigs of fresh dill Mayonnaise

SEAFOOD DRESSING

50 g mayonnaise 125 g. Sour cream

0.5 tsp. powdered sugar

1.0 tsp. ketchup

0.5 tsp. paprika

0.3 tsp. salt

0.5 tsp. lemon juice

2.0 tbsp. asparagus water or shrimp water

Remoulade

2 slices of white bread

Danish "Shooting Star" Open Face Sandwich - Stjerneskud

STEAMED PLAICE OR SOLE. Cut the plaice or sole down the body line and separate. Roll up the small half of your fillets and hold together with a toothpick. In a small pan pour the wine, water, salt and bring to a low boil. Add the 4 rolled fillets and using a lid, steam the rolls 1-2 minutes until barely cooked. Carefully pick up the fillets and place them on a plate with paper towels.

....

FRIED PLAICE OR SOLE. Whisk an egg together in a shallow bowl. Put the flour on a large plate. Spread the bread or Panko crumbs on another flat plate. First, salt and pepper each larger fillets on both sides. Then place both sides of each fillet in the flour first, then the egg and finally the bread or panko crumbs. Fry with lots of butter on a medium hot pan on both sides until golden brown. The fillets will continue to soak up the butter while frying, so keep adding butter to keep them from burning. When finished frying, place the fillets on a plate with a little paper towel.

.... SIDE DISHES

TO HAVE READY TO GO. Mix the ingredients for the dressing together in a bowl. Lightly steam the green asparagus in a small.

Danish "Shooting Star" Open Face Sandwich - Stjerneskud

saucepan, a little salty water. Don't overcook. Rinse and dry 4 lettuce leaves. Rinse the tomatoes and cut them in half. Hard boil 1 egg and quarter.

....

PLATING THE SANDWICH. Place on your serving plate, a half slice of buttered lightly toasted white bread. Then place a large lettuce leaf, letting the lettuce hang over the toast a bit. Lay your fried fillet on top. The fillet should almost cover the lettuce. If your fillets are too small you can add more fillet pieces to cover the lettuce. Put a large dollop of seafood sauce on the large end of the fried fillet and place the steamed rolled fillet and the roll of smoked lux on top. On the other end place a large dollop of remoulade, the arrange a couple of orderly rows of shrimp stacked. In the middle place 2 quartered eggs topped with a dollop each of red and black fish row. Place 2 steamed green asparagus across the eggs.

Optionally, you can place 4 asparagus, 2 green and 2 white. Garnish with dill sprigs, lemon, cucumber slices and tomato wedges or halved cherry tomatoes. It should look complicated but amazing. Your ready to serve!

Desserts

Danish Apple Cake - ./Eblekage

Danish Apple Cake - !Eblekage

This very traditional and old recipe was a favourite in our family. Old Farfar (Alfred) made this at special occasions. This recipe is best with good tart apples with lots of flavour like Granny Smith apples... so let's be clear, this desert is all about the apples! If you want to take this desert to the next level, then make your own bread crumbs from great tasting white bread. Tip, you can make this dessert the day before, just don't add the whipped cream and jelly until just before serving.

APPLE SAUCE:

1 kg (2.2 lbs) peeled, cored sliced tart apples (Granny Smith)

50 g (1/4 cup) butter

115 g (1/2 cup) of water

130 g (.6 cup) packed brown sugar

2 tsp premium vanilla extract 1/2 tsp lemon juice

BREAD CRUMBS:

120 g (1 1/2 cups) fresh bread crumbs

115 g (1/2 cup) butter

20 g (1/8 cup) white sugar

WHIPPING CREAM:

475 g (2 cups) heavy cream 25 g (1/8 cup) white sugar

2 tsp premium vanilla extract 5 tsp size blobs of red currant jelly

THE APPLE SAUCE:. Put the apples and butter into a large pot and cook using medium heat for a couple of minutes. Add the water, brown sugar, vanilla extract and lemon juice. Mix well and simmer at a low boil for 10 minutes or until the apples are soft. Roughly, mash the apples with a fork leaving small chunks in the sauce, then set aside in the fridge to cool.

Yield: serves 10 I Recipe by Kim Sorensen

Danish Apple Cake - !Eblekage

THE BREAD CRUMBS:. In a large frying pan melt butter over medium heat, then add the bread crumbs and sugar, stirring slowly and continually till the golden brown. Spread the bread crumbs on a cookie sheet to cool. Beware: bread crumbs can burn in seconds, so don't take your eyes off them.

....

THE WHIPPED CREAM:. Pour the heavy cream, sugar and vanilla extract into your mixer bowl and whip at high speed till thick and fluffy.

....

ASSEMBLING THE SERVING BOWL:. In the bottom of your serving bowl, put and level flat 1/3 of your apple sauce, followed by a thin flat layer (1/8") of bread crumbs. Put the remaining apple sauce (2/3) on top followed by another layer (1/4") of bread crumbs. Now cover the top with a thick layer of whipped cream. Lastly, place 4-6 small blobs of the jelly on top for garnishing. Best serve chilled.

Almond Rice Pudding - Ris a'lamande

This is the most traditional Danish dessert. It's almost always served at Christmas, but also served throughout the year at special occasions. If you can't find Bing cherries in the can, you can use fresh or frozen cherries. Tip #1: You want a really soft textured rice, so don't wait til the rice has absorbed all the milk and cream... put it in the serving bowl a wee bit wet. Then fold in the whipping cream as soon as the rice has cooled. Tip #2: In my opinion the sauce is everything, so make sure you have a great tasting sauce. I like the sweet and sour cherry taste. You can find a sour cherry syrup in most European grocery stores. Tip #3: Also don't make the sauce too thick. It should run a little.

THE RICE

2 cups Arborio rice

1 cup water

2 cups milk

2 cups heavy cream

3 tbsp vanilla extract

4 tbsp sugar

1/4 tsp salt

THE WHIPPING CREAM

2 cups whipping cream 4 tbsp sugar

3 tsp almond extract **THE CHERRY SAUCE**

796 ml (3 1/3 cup) Can of Bing Cherries plus the 1/2 cup of the light syrup

3 tbl sugar

1 tbl fresh lemon juice 1 tbl butter

1 cup sour cherry syrup 1 tbl cornstarch

1/4 cup water

1/2 tsp pure almond extract

Yield: serves 10 I Recipe by Kim Sorensen

Almond Rice Pudding - Ris a'lamande

For the rice... in a rice cooker, boil the water with the rice and salt. When the water is almost gone add the milk, heavy cream, vanilla extract, sugar. Let simmer in the cooker until the milk and cream are almost absorbed. Remove rice into a bowl and place on the counter to cool. It should be wet, not dry.

....

For the whipping cream... place in a mixing bowl the heavy cream, sugar and almond extract. Then beat the cream till stiff. Fold into the rice as soon as it is cool enough to do so. Then place into the fridge until you're ready to serve. Tip... too much rice and its too heavy... too much whipping cream and its too light.

....

The cherry sauce... Place the cherries, liquid, sugar, lemon and almond extract in a pot and bring to a slow boil. Add the sour cherry syrup before adding the dissolved cornstarch and slow boil till sauce is thicken.

....

Putting the Ris a'lamonde together... Remove the rice from the fridge. The mixture should be soft and fluffy. Serve with cherry sauce and garnished with a fresh mint sprig.

Almond Rice Pudding - Ris a'lamande

Danish Lemon Mousse - Citronfromage

An old family favourite of Doris and Alfred Sorensen. Everyone will enjoy this one!

4 eggs - yolks/whites separated 125 g (1/2 cup) of lemon juice zest from 2 lemons

100 g (1/2 cup) sugar

120 g (1/2 cup) hot water

1 envelope of Knox gelatin

1 cup of whipping cream

2 tbsp of sugar

Separate the eggs, placing the egg yolks in your intended serving bowl and the egg whites in your mixing bowl. Set aside the egg whites in the mixing bowl to beat later. In your intended "serving" bowl whisk the yokes with the sugar until very light in colour. In a pot on your stove top mix 1 envelope of Knox gelatin in the hot/warm water till dissolved, then add the juice and the zest from the lemons. After cooling, mix together with the egg and sugar in the "serving" bowl and set aside in the fridge so it can just begin to set (15-20 min) (don't let it set too much or you will have difficulty folding in the whipped cream and egg whites). Whip the whipping cream and sugar in a bowl and set aside. Beat the egg whites in your mixing bowl fluffy and stiff. Check the mixture in the fridge, once the mixture BEGINS to set remove from fridge and fold in the whip cream and the egg whites. Place back in the fridge to set for a couple of hours.

Yield: serves 6 - 8 I Recipe by Kim Sorensen

Danish Lemon Mousse - Citronfromage

When ready whip up a little more whipping cream and sugar for garnishing. Then dish up a serving in a bowl and garnish with a dollop of whipped cream and a mint leaf. You can also, after folding, pour the mixture directly into individual serving bowls and then let them set in the fridge before serving with the same garnish.

Danish Raspberry Pudding - Hindbaer Fromage

This is an easy to make dessert with a powerful sweet raspberry taste. You can use raspberry juice, frozen raspberries or fresh raspberries, but fresh raspberries is by far the best. If possible, filter out the seeds as they can be annoying.

300 g (2 cups) pureed raspberries

1 pkge of gelatin (1/4 cup) hot water

(1/2 cup) water

100 g (2/3 cup) sugar

1 cup heavy cream

2 tbsp sugar

In a medium size pot dissolve the gelatin in a 1/4 cup of hot water. Then, in a blender, add 1/2 cup of water, raspberries and sugar and blend well. Using a fine screen stainer, filter out just the seeds and then pour the blended mixture into the pot of dissolved gelatin, mix well and pour into a large serving bowl. Place bowl in the fridge to cool until it just starts to set (about 15-20 minutes). While you're waiting for the mixture to set, whip 1 cup of heavy cream with 2 tbl of sugar. Once the mixture has just started to set, fold the whipped cream into the mixture until smooth with no lumps. Now either leave the mixture in the large serving bowl or pour the mixture into individual ramekins before placing in the fridge to complete its setting. Add a dollop of sweeten whipped cream (with a little vanilla extract) with one whole raspery and mint leaf as garnish.

Yield: serves 6 I Recipe by Kim Sorensen

Red Fruit Pudding Dessert - Rodgrod med Flore

This is a very old recipe and very quick and easy to make. It's direct translation is ,Red Porridge with Cream,. You can use any combination of 500 g of strawberries, raspberries, black and1or red currants, rhubarb or cherries. Frozen fruit works great, but freshly picked is best! Better tasting fruit means better tasting Rodgrod! Ya, it's simple to make but the best part is it's so delicious!

500 g (18 oz) of any combination of strawberry, raspberry, black currant, red currant, rhubarb or cherries 150 g (4.5 oz) sugar
2 tsp vanilla extract

250 g (1 cup) water
2 tbsp potato or corn starch (dissolved in 5 tbsp water) Whipping Cream

Cut the fruit into dime size small chunks. Transfer all the ingredients except the potato starch into a saucepan and mix well. Slow boil the berries and water mixture for 10 minutes. Add the dissolved potato starch and lower the heat to a simmer for another 5 minutes. Barely boil it. Then pour the pudding into 4 dishes and let it cool off before serving it with cold heavy cream.

Yield: Makes 4 servings I Recipe by Kim Sorensen

Danish Ring Cake - Danish Kransekage

This is Denmarks most unique and recognizable cake. The origin of the Kransekage can be traced back to the 18th century, where it was first created by a baker in Copenhagen. It soon evolved into a curvy horn and was laid on its side and appropriately called the "Horn Of Plenty" (Overfludighedshorn). It was to give thanks for the years harvest and it was appropriately filled with the bounty of the harvest and sometimes with candies or both. Eventually, because of the religious society, the Kransekage evolved into an upright cake, that some say represented a church steeple and was more appropriate for church weddings than the Horn of Plenty. It was said to represent everlasting or never-ending loving relationships. Today the Kransekage is used for many different occasions, weddings, anniversaries, birthdays, special days like New Years or any special event. Kransekage is a series of concentric rings of cake, layered on top of each other in order to form a steep-sloped cone shape-often 18 or more layers-stuck together with white icing. Kransekage cake rings are made with almonds paste, sugar, and egg whites. Our family started a tradition where the bride and groom together lift the top layer of the cake at their wedding. The number of cake rings that stick to the top one when they lift it is said to be the number of children the couple will have. Hmmm, good luck with that one! After the bride and groom have fed each other a piece of the cake, they pile the pieces onto a tray, then make their way around the room, offering a piece to each of the guests. In Danish tradition, it means good luck for the bride and groom, if every guest at the wedding tastes a piece of their cake. You can also sometimes find a fine bottle of wine in the middle of the cake for some Anniversary and Wedding ones.

Regardless of the event, when you see one of these beautifully decorated cakes, you just know there is something special going on!!

Danish Ring Cake - Danish Kransekage

My aunt Elsie made this cake for our family for decades and now others, especially my wife Marnie, have taken up this task for the family. Elsie's only hard rule was that you had to use Coop brand ground almonds because it was the best! Hmm, all I know is that the ideal Kransekage is barely gold in colour and slightly firm to the touch, yet soft and chewy in the center.

....

The picture below is a new style where the ring is more upright than round. There are many variations today that include using chocolate icing, edible flowers and an amazing variety of decorations. It's endless what can be done to a Kransekage cake, but they all are make of marzipan.

Marnie's Kransekage Cake for Mom's 90th birthday!

Danish Ring Cake - Danish Kransekage

1000 g Odense almond
paste 200 g sugar

60 g egg white
2 tsp almond extract

In a large bowl and using your fist, knead the Odense almond paste with the sugar. Then add the egg whites and continue kneading until well mixed. Cover with plastic wrap and place in the fridge for 6 hours or overnight. Using your dusted hands, roll your dough out on a lightly dusted (very fine flour like potato flour) counter top into even size rolls... about 1/2 to 3/4 inch in diameter. Now start making your 18 rings using your Kransekage ring pans. Use your hands to connect the ends and smooth out the joint. Carefully turn each ring upside on parchment paper maintaining the perfect symmetrical circle. Place the rings and parchment paper on a cookie sheet and place in the oven set at 350 F in the Bake setting (not convection) for approximately 15 minutes depending on how hot your oven is. Regardless, pull the Kransekage out as soon as it has turned slightly beige or lightly golden.

....

If you're using the "From Scratch Recipe", mix all the ingredients well and follow the same steps as described above. Mixing Kransekage from scratch is not easy, so good luck!

Recipe by "Inspired by Elsie Stoyberg"

Danish Ring Cake - Danish Kransekage

FROM SCRATCH RECIPE

500 g co-op brand ground almonds

2 cups sugar

1/4 tsp almond oil

2/3 -3/4 cup egg white

TIP#1 Baking the rings directly on parchment paper and a cookie sheet, will prevent the rings from sticking or breaking compared to what generally happens when trying to remove them from the metal rings. TIP#2 If you don't want any browning on the bottom of your rings, use a grill between the parchment paper and the cookie tray. TIP#3 Do not use the convection setting as this will bake too fast and brown parts of the rings before cooking the inside.

TIP#4 Make sure to bring the dough up to room temperature before placing them in the oven. This will also help cook the inside while not brown too much on the outside. In the end your Kransekage must be slightly beige on the outside and soft and barely cooked on the inside. TIP#5 Do a test bake on your first ring to check the heat and and time needed for perfect Kransekage!

Recipe by Aunt Elsie

Danish Ring Cake - Danish Kransekage

3 cups icing sugar 2 egg white

2 tsp vinegar

1 tsp vanilla extract

Combine the sugar, egg white, and vanilla extract to make a nice and delicious frosting that will serve as both decorative and glue for the rings. Organize the rings by size. Place the frosting in a piping bag and pipe swirly pattern on each dough ring (see picture). Assemble the cake by stacking each dough ring on top of each other, using the frosting/icing as glue. We use equal amounts of Danish and Canadian flags but you can use other flags as well. Continue to decorate with anything appropriate for the occasion, It's endless what can be used to decorate this Kransekage tower!

So have fun with it.

Danish Pastry - Wienerbrod

Danish pastries can take many forms and have become the world standard for pastries. This one is our family favourite and could be arguably the best of the best. This recipe comes from the legendary Black Diamond Baker, George Nielsen. This pastry has been available in the Calgary area for over 40 years! All the ingredients can be bought from stores, although the Barvarian Cream maybe a challenge. I buy Barvarian Cream from the commercial Baker's store in Calgary. The problem is, it only comes in a large commercial quantities. Tip #1 - the day before, place the flour in the fridge or better yet, in the freezer and the butter in the fridge. Both must be cold. Tip #2 - This recipe makes 16 pastries because that will use up the plastic bag of Bavarian Cream. Once you open up the bag, it will not keep for very long, so you might as well make all 16 pastries up in one go. You can freeze each pastry that you do not right away. When you need one, just thaw, let rise and then add the hazel nuts and sugar and bake at 350 F for 25 minutes and just like that, you have an amazing Wienerbrod!

THE DOUGH	THE FILLING
1048 g Bread Flour	454 g Almond
454 g Pastry Flour	Paste 227 g
112 g Sugar	White Cake
112 g Butter	681 g Sugar
260 g (4) Eggs	681 g Baker's
800 g Water	Margarine
150 g Fresh Yeast	Bavarian Cream
	Hazelnuts
	Ground Cardamom
	1 Tbsp Almond Extract

Yield: 16 - 10" x 4" pastries I Recipe by George Nielsen

Danish Pastry - Wienerbrod

First make the filling so it is ready to go when needed. Add the almond paste and sugar until the paste has absorbed the sugar. Slowly add in chunks of white cake. Once the cake has been mixed in, slowly add chunks of butter and almond extract. Don't over mix, otherwise you'll get to much air in the mixture. Set aside (in the fridge) until needed. In your mixer, add the cold flour, sugar and salt and mix together. In a separate container, whisk the yeast, egg and water together. Add 3/4 of this mixture to your mixer machine and start mixing. After mixing for a minute, and the rest of the water mixture and continue mixing. Immediately, while mixing, dust the sides of the mixer with more flour (1/2 to 1 cup of flour). Don't over mix. The dough will be slightly sticky and the sides of the mixer will not be clean. Sprinkle flour on the counter and remove the dough from the mixer to the counter and start kneading for a few minutes, finishing with a round ball of dough. Take a large rolling pin and flatten the four sides of the dough out at least 8" leaving a hill of dough in the middle. Knead and roll the butter a few times and then flatten to about a 6" x 6" size and place on top of the dough hill. Pull the rolled out dough edges over the butter.

Danish Pastry - Wienerbrod

Roll the dough flat to approximately 24" x 12". Fold the left and right sides of the dough and repeat this process three times. Let it sit 10 minutes semi flatten before you roll it out to 24" x 12" for the last time.

Total number of rolls and folds is three times. Brush any excess crumbs or flour off the dough. Using a measuring tape, cut the dough so you have two pieces 6" x 24". Then cut each piece 3" wide for a total of 16 - 3" x 6" equal pieces. Now roll each piece out to a 12" x 6" rectangle by rolling them gently and without pressing down to hard. Use lots of flour on your counter so the dough doesn't stick. Once they are rolled out, using a brush remove any excess flour or crumbs. Now using a long flat spreader, add the almond filling (approx. 100 g or 3.6 oz) the length of each wienerbrod about 1" width. Then add a layer of Bavarian Cream (approx. 1,400 g or 50 oz) Sprinkle about 1 - 2 tsp of Cardamom on top. Fold one side of the dough on top of the filling. Brush the tip of that side and the whole of the unfolded side of dough with water. This seals the pastry. Fold over the second side and using your fingers, press the top down to secure. Clean the pastry with brush to get rid of any excess flour or crumbs.

Danish Pastry - Wienerbrod

Brush the top of the pastry with water again. Proof in an oven with proofing ability until it has risen double in size. It helps to put very hot water in the oven when proofing to keep the humidity high. Once proofed, sprinkle the middle top lengthwise with crushed hazelnuts (1/3 C) and white sugar (1/8 C). Bake at 350 F for about 25 minutes.

www.ingramcontent.com/pod-product-compliance
Lightning Source LLC
Chambersburg PA
CBHW041139120626
46547CB00020B/3049